New Revised Edition!!!

Blackjack...Y_____ only casino game which a_____ n edge over the casino. Eas_____ ___ basic card counting can show you how to be one of the 5% who are a winner...

Craps... This is the fastest and most exciting of the casino games and one which allows you to win the most money in the shortest period of time. We'll show you the bets which give the house no edge whatsoever and how to use these bets toward a winning approach at craps...

Video Poker... The new, exciting casino game pits a player's skills and decision-making against the machine. You'll learn the different types of games available, how to play, the payoffs and the best strategies to follow to win the giant jackpots...

Poker... This is the most fascinating gambling game and combines skill, luck and psychology, an intriguing combination which draws millions of players to card tables to try their hand. Learn how to play and win at the most popular poker games...

Keno... You may be one step closer to winning a $50,000 jackpot after reading this chapter. Learn how to play and how to win, the house odds and the best playing strategies for all the different keno tickets available...

Slots... We'll show you the "insider" secrets - how to find the casinos and the machines with the largest and most frequent payoffs. Learn all about straight, progressive and specialty slots, and the winning approaches...

Roulette... Learn all about this exciting and glamorous game which has attracted kings and queens, captains of industry and millionaires from around the world. We'll show you the great variety of bets available, the different payoffs and the most important winning systems available...

BEAT THE ODDS

How To Win at Gambling!

J. Edward Allen

*One of the Best All-Around Books on Beating the Casino.
Take it From Me, This is a Great Book."*
Avery Cardoza, Best-Selling Gambling Author

- Gambling Research Institute -
Cardoza Publishing

CARDOZA PUBLISHING, publisher of **Gambling Research Institute** (GRI) books, is the foremost gaming and gambling publisher in the world with a library of more than 50 up-to-date books and strategies on winning. These easy-to-read works are written by the top experts and authorities in their fields, and with more than 4,500,000 in print, represent the best-selling and most popular gaming books anywhere.

PRINTING HISTORY

First Printing	March 1987
Second Printing	August 1988
First Revised Edition	June 1991

New, Revised Edition
August 1993
May 1994

ISBN:0-940685-41-8
Library of Congress Catalogue Card Number: 93-70983
Cover Photos by Ron Charles

See back pages for information on ordering advanced winning strategies. With your order, you'll receive our free catalogue of gaming books, advanced strategies and computer games. Or you may request the free catalogue by itself at the address below.

Call or write for information on bulk purchases of this book.

CARDOZA PUBLISHING
P.O. Box 1500, Cooper Station, New York, NY 10276
(718)743-5229

Table of Contents

One. Introduction

Learn to beat the odds! If you want to gamble, then you should be as well informed as possible, and in this book, we'll give you all the information necessary to enable you to make the best bets and play the best strategies. Instead of playing against the odds, you'll play like a winner. And that's what this book is all about — playing to win!

You not only learn the fundamentals of playing and winning at all the forms of gambling we cover, but also, money management and self-control methods, which allows you to play like a pro and retain those winnings. There's a wealth of knowledge in this book, and our aim is to make you a respected player and a winner.

All our sections are written in an easy-to-understand style, and are fully illustrated with pictures, tables and charts, so that any beginner, novice or experienced player can follow the information presented to beat the odds.

The first game we cover is blackjack, by far the most popular of the table games offered by the casino. The reason for this popularity is simple: it's the only game in the house where the player can have an edge over the casino.

We cover the basic strategies necessary to master the game. Our strategies are based on computer studies, and will point the way for you to become a professional blackjack player.

Our second game, craps, is certainly the fastest and most exciting of the casino table games. There is action on every roll of the dice, and it's a game in which you can let loose and show your emotions openly, especially when things are going green, and winnings are piling onto winnings.

We cover the game simply and clearly, so that you fully understand how to play craps, which are the best bets to make, and which wagers should be avoided at all costs.

Video Poker is becoming the latest casino craze for skill is involved and proper play can make one a winner. In our comprehensive coverage we'll show you how to play the various types of machines, the different options you have available, and the best strategies to follow to beat the video poker machines!

You'll learn all there is to know about video poker for this section is chock-full of information, facts and figures to make you a competent player and a winner at this exciting new game.

The next game we cover, poker, may be the greatest game invented by man, for it combines skill, luck and psychology. Best of all, it can be played in a card club, casino or privately, and once you have mastered the game, there is nothing but money to be made.

We discuss the most popular of the poker games -7 Card Stud, Lowball, Draw Poker and Texas Hold'Em.

This section is a little gem, for, after reading it, you can go out and hold your own against top players.

Keno is a game that has attracted millions of players for a very good reason. With just a small bet, less than a dollar in most cases, and some luck, a player can walk away with thousands of dollars, and might even hit that $50,000 payoff if lady luck really shines on him or her.

We'll show you all the different bets that can be made in keno, a number of which only the top pros know about, and you'll soon see why millions are attracted to this game.

In our section on slots, you'll learn how to play the game for the best odds, what machines to play on, plus a full history of the slot machine, all of which makes for fascinating reading. Find out how odds are figured and how slots are set up in a casino so that all this information can be used to your advantage.

We reveal inside information on slots, and after reading this section, you'll not only be an informed player, but hopefully, a winner as well.

The last game covered, roulette, has fascinated and intrigued millions of players over the years. It's not only a leisurely game to play, but an exciting one as well. You'll be able to play roulette in the same manner as kings, queens, statesmen and millionaires have over the years.

Roulette has a great variety of bets available, and we discuss all of them in detail. Both the American and European game are fully covered so that no matter where you find yourself, you can make the best bets at this ancient and interesting game. And with a little luck, you may come home with big winnings.

Let's beat the odds!

Two. Blackjack

1. Introduction

Blackjack's popularity continues to grow, and it is by far the most popular of the table games the casino offers. The reason for this is simple: it's the only game in the house where the player can have an edge over the house.

In order to have this edge, the player must know basic strategy and play this strategy correctly. But that's not difficult to do, and it's all here in this guide—everything the player must know to play at his best and to beat the house.

The strategies shown in this book are based upon computer studies and should be studied carefully. They're explained so that anyone, after a few hours or less of practice, can be a winner at blackjack.

The book is written in simple and clear language, and its one purpose is in making you, the reader, a winner at this most popular and exciting casino game.

2. The Blackjack Scene

The arca devoted to blackjack in any casino will usually be the largest area devoted to any of the table games, which include not only blackjack, but craps, roulette and baccarat. In fact, in many casinos the game is so popular that several areas may offer the game of blackjack.

It's therefore not hard to find a game when entering the casino. There will be a number of tables placed so that they surround a center area from which the casino personnel operate. This is known as the **blackjack pit**.

The Table

The blackjack table is a modified oval, with the seats arranged around the curved portion. There will be as many seats available as spots on the table.

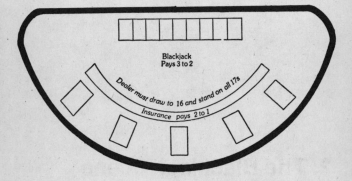

The number of seats available at a blackjack table ranges from five to seven depending upon the casino. While the players remain seated throughout the game (unless they wish to stand) the dealer stands and faces them from the inside of the pit.

Directly in front of the dealer is the chip rack, containing the casino chips. To his right (sometimes to his left) is a slot where cash is dropped when players come to the table and change cash for chips.

Also on the table may be a **shoe** which is a rectangular box, either made of plastic or wood, which holds at least four decks of cards. If the game is played with only one or two decks, there will be no shoe on the table.

There may also be a small sign stating the minimum bet (and sometimes the maximum one) permitted at the table. Sometimes this small sign shows additional rules, other than those imprinted on the green felt covering the table.

The green felt contains boxes where each player will place his chips for betting purposes, and where usually two or three rules of the game are printed. The most common is *Dealer Must Draw to 16, and Stand on All 17s*, which refers to the totals of the points the dealer holds. The next most common rule is *Insurance Pays 2-1*. The third is *Blackjack Pays 3-2*.

These are very basic rules that we need not concern ourselves with right now, for they will be fully explained at the appropriate time.

The Dealer

Unlike the players, the dealer stands throughout the game, and wears the house uniform. In these days of tighter security, there is usually some name tag and sometimes a picture of the dealer attached, so that the players can, by looking closely, ascertain the name of the dealer.

The dealer runs the game. He changes cash into chips issued by the casino; he **changes color**—that is, changing casino chips into smaller or larger denominations. He shuffles the cards, and deals them out. He pays off winning bets and collects losing bets. He answers questions of the players, and is there to help them, as well as run the game.

Tipping the Dealer

Tipping, or **toking** the dealer, to use a casino term, is not required, but is often done. Some players overtip; others never tip at all. And some, if they tip, don't do it correctly.

A dealer should be toked if you feel that he or she has been friendly and helpful, and has made your game more enjoyable. In that case, every now and then you can make a bet for the dealer by putting out a chip above your box in the area marked for insurance bets.

When you do this, if you win your bet, the dealer will win his; if you lose, the dealer will also lose. The dealers prefer this kind of toking, for it gives them the chance to double the original bet, and sometimes win even more if the player is dealt a blackjack.

Sometimes players tip after a blackjack is dealt to them, but one must remember that no matter how generous you want to be, your edge at blackjack is very slight, and overtipping will erode your winnings. Strike a happy balance, but under no circumstances tip a hostile or unfriendly dealer, or one who wants you to lose and considers you a sucker for playing.

The Casino Chips

Casino personnel call chips **checks**, but we're going to use the term chips throughout this book because it's the most popular term, understood by all players.

These are issued by a casino in standard denominations; usually for $1, $5, $25, and $100. Some casinos have $500 and even higher denomination chips, and many casinos have 50¢ chips at the blackjack table, because payoffs are often in this amount. There are casinos that don't bother issuing chips this small, and instead pay off with coins, either half-dollars or quarters. In some of the Northern Nevada casinos, $2.50 chips are used at the blackjack tables, saving the dealers time and trouble when payoffs for $5 blackjacks are made. A blackjack, which will be explained later, pays 3-2, and a $5 wager will be paid off with $7.50.

Players can also play with cash, but casino executives frown on this. Some players like to play only in cash, but if they win they'll have to settle for casino chips as their payoff. Dealers will always pay off in casino chips, not in cash.

Casinos have minimum betting limits, which usually are $1 or $2. Some tables may have $5 or $25 or even higher minimum limits, because *high rollers* don't want to be betting thousands while some other player is betting $2 at a time.

After you leave a table, you can cash in your casino chips at the **cashier's cage** of the casino. If you don't spot it, any security guard or other casino personnel will show you where it is. That's where you get cash for your chips, not at the blackjack table.

The Players

Even though there may be five to seven spots open for players at any blackjack table, the game will begin if one player shows up to play. When more than one player is at a table, additional players can take any of the vacant seats. There is no set rule where one is to sit.

The cards are dealt, as we shall see, in a clockwise fashion so that the player to the dealer's left, facing him, is the first player to receive cards. He is known as the **first baseman**. The player at the other end of the table, nearest to the dealer's right, is the last player to receive cards, and he's known as the **third baseman** or **anchorman.**

Where should one sit at a table if given the choice? Most experts prefer either the third baseman's seat or the one to its right, for they get a look at the other hands before they have to make any playing decisions.

But if you're a beginner, don't sit in the third baseman's seat. You might feel too much pressure, for sometimes when you draw a card you'll inadvertently make the dealer a winner. Even though you made the right decision, ignorant players may unfairly blame you for their losses. But, as you get more expert, sit as close to the third baseman's seat as you can, for you get that little extra information playing last.

Players in casino blackjack play their hands as individuals, trying to beat the dealer, not each other. When you are dealt cards, all you want to do is get a better hand than the dealer, so you can win. The other hands are immaterial to this result, and often some players at the table will win a hand while others will be losing their hands.

3. The Cards and Rules of Play

The Cards

A standard deck of 52 cards is used in the game of casino blackjack. At one time most games were played with this single deck of cards, but today there are many multiple deck games in existence. But no matter how many decks are used, whether two or eight, they are merely multiples of the standard 52 deck game. Therefore, if a player is at a table where two decks are used, the dealer is using 104 cards, made up of two standard decks of 52 cards each.

The standard deck of cards contains four suits; clubs, diamonds, hearts and spades. In blackjack, the suits have no material value and can be disregarded. What is important is the value of the cards.

Value of the Cards

Each of the four suits contains the identical 13

cards, ranging from an ace to a king. The cards are ace, 2, 3, 4, 5, 6, 7, 8, 9, 10, jack, queen and king.

In casino blackjack, the following cards are counted as 10s, and have that value for adding purposes to ascertain the total of the hand: 10, jack, queen and king.

In the future, we'll refer to any of these cards as a **10-value card** or simply as a **10**. There are sixteen 10-value cards in the standard deck, and therefore these are the most frequent cards in play. All the other values consist of only four cards.

To value a card, other than the ace, which we'll write about last, we simply examine the spots on the card, as well as the numerical value in the form of a number at the corners. Thus a 2 has two spots, the 3 three, the 4 four, and all the way up to the 9, which has 9 spots.

The ace is the most powerful card in blackjack, and one of the reasons for its importance is that it can be valued, at the option of the player, as either a 1 or 11.

Blackjack is also called **21** because that is the highest total that a player may validly hold. Any hand totaling more than 21 points is a loser, and so called a **"bust."** The ace, which can be valued at 1 or 11, sometimes prevents hands from going over 21, or "busting"—that is, losing, when it is valued as a 1.

For example, a hand containing 10-3-ace is merely a 14, not a 24, because the player simply values the ace as a 1. The ace gives players, especially beginners, the most trouble. Often they think they've busted, or lost, because they value the ace as an 11 instead of as a 1. If in doubt, show the hand to the dealer and let him value it for you.

Object of the Game

When we discuss the object of the game, we write about the object from the player's standpoint. The dealer has no object to his play; he simply must follow the rules set forth by the casino, which is to stand on hands of 17 or more, and draw to all hands of 16 or less.

The object of the game, in its most simple terms, is to beat the dealer. To do this, the player can win in two ways. First of all, he or she must have a total higher than the dealer's total, or he or she must have a valid hand, of whatever total, while the dealer "busts" or goes over 21.

The player loses if his or her total is less than the dealer's total, or if the player busts. Once the player busts, his hand is out of play and his bet is removed. It doesn't matter to this player if the dealer subsequently busts his own hand; once the player busts, he loses.

If both the player and the dealer have the same totals in their respective hands, it's a tie, a standoff. The casino term for this is a **"push."** And that's just what it is, a push. Neither the player nor the dealer win.

How does a player improve his total? First, to understand this concept, we have to look at the original hand dealt to the player.

The Original Hand

The dealer, to put a round of play in motion, deals out two cards to each of the players and two cards to himself. The cards are dealt one at a time, face down, the player to the dealer's left getting the first card, and then each player after that getting a card in clockwise fashion. After each player has received one card, then the dealer gives himself a card, also face down. Then a second card is dealt to each of the players, also face down, in the same order, and the dealer gets his second card, and turns it face up.

This face up card is known as the **upcard**. Thus, all the players see one of the dealer's cards, but the dealer sees none of the players' cards. It wouldn't matter if he saw the players' cards or not, for the dealer, as we have said, is bound by strict rules. In some casinos, in multiple deck games, the players' cards are dealt face up.

Most players prefer to have their cards dealt face down, for it gives them a feeling they're actually involved in a secret game of some sort, hiding their cards from the dealer, who couldn't care less. But most experts prefer to see all the cards dealt face up, because they get a better grasp of what cards are in play and out of the deck, and this gives them a slight advantage.

The two cards the player gets at the outset of play is an original hand. The highest total he can get is 21 on on original hand; an ace and a 10-value card. When a player (or dealer) gets this hand, it's known as a **blackjack**, or a **natural**. A blackjack pays 3-2 if it wins. All other winning hands pay even-money. If a dealer gets a blackjack and none of the players have a blackjack, the dealer simply wins the player's bet at even-money; he doesn't get that extra bonus.

If a player and the dealer have a blackjack, then it's a push; neither win.

The next highest total is a 20. This is a very strong hand, and usually a winning one, either on the part of the dealer or the player. Thereafter, the hands go down in value.

The important thing to remember is that neither a player nor a dealer can bust on the original hand. The following are some original hands and their totals:

Hand	Total
queen-5	15
9-8	17
4-8	12
10-king	20
ace-8	19

Hitting and Standing

If a player wants to improve his hand, he can draw a card to that hand. This is called **hitting** or **drawing**. For example, if a player is dealt a 5-3, his total is only 8. Even if he hits the hand, he can't bust, or go over 21. So he hits the hand, not worrying about busting.

If a player is dealt a 10-king, he has a total of 20. He doesn't want to hit this hand, for his total is very strong, just one below the highest possible total, and if hc hits the hand he will bust unless he gets an ace, and the odds against getting one of the four aces is very high indeed, so he stands.

Hard and Soft Totals

Any hand that doesn't contain an ace is a **hard** hand, and the total of those hard hands are **hard totals**. Most of the hands dealt to either the player or the dealer will be hard hands like these.

Some examples of hard hands:

5-4, which is a hard 9.
10-5, which is a hard 15.
Jack-king, which is a hard 20.

There is another way to have a hard hand, and that is to have a hand containing an ace, where the ace is counted as 1, not as an 11. For example, suppose the player were dealt an original hand of 10-4, and hit it and got an ace. He now would have hard 15, because he must value the ace as 1. If he valued it as an 11, the hand would total 25 and bust.

Other hard hands containing an ace:

10-6-ace, which is a hard 17.
9-4-ace, which is a hard 14.
8-3-ace, which is a hard 12.

Any hand which contains an ace that is valued at 11, rather than as 1, is a **soft** hand, and its total is a **soft total**.

For example, suppose a player received an original hand of ace-9. It would be a soft 20, with the ace counted as an 11. Of course, the player would have the option of counting the hand a 10, but that would be foolish, since his 20 is very strong, and if he counted it as a 10 and hit the hand, any card drawn other than an ace or ten-value would weaken the hand.

Here are some examples of soft hands:

ace-9 is a soft 20.

ace-8 is a soft 19.

ace-7 is a soft 18.

A soft hand has one important advantage. Even if the hand is hit, it can't bust. So if a foolish player hit a soft 20, consisting of an ace and 9, he still coudn't bust.

A soft hand can become a hard hand, if it's drawn to. For example, if a player were dealt an ace-6 for a soft 17 and hit and got an 8, his hand would now be a hard 15 (ace-6-8 = 15). An ace-4, which is a soft 15, if hit with a 7, would become a hard 12. But the same ace-4, if hit with a 5, would become a soft 20.

We'll go into the strategies of hitting or standing on soft totals later on.

The Blackjack

This is the strongest of all hands, and consists of an ace and a 10-value card (10, jack, queen or king) dealt as an original hand. It is an immediate winner for the player—unless the dealer has a blackjack also, in which case it is a push. But if the dealer doesn't have a blackjack, it pays off at 3-2.

If the dealer has a blackjack and none of the players have one, then the dealer wins all the bets at the table.

As we shall see, the player has an option of splitting aces and playing each ace as a separate hand. If a ten-value card is dealt to a split ace, it's not a blackjack, just a 21.

Remember, only an ace and a 10-value card in the original hand is a blackjack.

Busting

Sometimes this is also known as **breaking**, but busting is the more common term used in casinos. When either a player or a dealer has drawn cards to his or her original hand and gone over 21, the hand is a losing one; for he or she has busted. The only valid hands are those of 21 or fewer points.

When we bust—that is, go over 21 after hitting our hand—we must turn the cards over immediately to show that we lost, and the dealer will, at that point, take away both our cards and our chips. We've lost, and are out of the game for that round of play, even if the dealer subsequently busts. This is the really big edge the casino has over us. If the dealer and the player both bust, the player still loses.

Well, then, you might ask, why would anyone risk drawing and busting a hand? As we shall see, there are times when the dealer's upcard forces us to hit our hand, even though we may bust, because he probably has a 17 or higher total, and if we stand with a **stiff** total, or 12 to 16, we'll lose our bets without even trying to improve our hands.

4. Playing the Casino Game

We're now ready to see how the game is played in a casino. For purposes of this illustration, we're going to assume we enter a casino to play some 21. The first thing we do is head for the blackjack pit, and look for a table that will accommodate our wagers. If we wish to bet only $2 a hand, we must find a table with a $1 or $2 minimum, and avoid the tables with a $5 or higher minimum.

We find several tables like that, and at one table only two other players are seated, one in the first baseman's spot at the extreme left of the dealer. The other player is in the center spot, so we move to the anchorman's seat and take out some cash, place it on the table, and wait for the dealer to change this into casino chips.

The dealer is about to shuffle up the cards, and so he puts them down and takes our cash. Our involvement with casino blackjack is about to begin.

Changing Cash into Chips

We are already seated in the last chair when the dealer takes our cash and counts it. We had put down $40, in assorted $10s and $20s, and the dealer will turn the money over after counting it, to verify that it's not *funny money* with one denomination printed on the front and a different one printed on the back.

In most casinos, he'll not only verify the amount with us by announcing *forty dollars*, but will try and catch the attention of a casino executive, a floorman, who will be in the interior of the pit, supervising the games. After the floorman acknowledges that this cash amount is being exchanged for chips, the dealer will drop the cash into a slot and it will disappear from view.

Then he'll give us $40 worth of chips. Since it's a $2 table, he might give us $20 worth of $1 chips and four $5 chips. We count the chips after he gives them to us. Anyone can make a mistake, and this is perfectly acceptable behavior.

While we're doing this, the dealer is shuffling the cards.

Shuffling, Cutting and Burning a Card

In the casino we're playing at, there are both one-deck and multiple-deck games, but we've sat at a table with a one-deck game. The dealer is shuffling up the cards, doing a thorough job. When he's finished, the cards are placed on the table in front of one of the players to be cut. Some players, out of superstition, refuse to cut the cards, which is also acceptable. But the player sitting in the first base cuts them by taking up a portion of the cards and placing them next to the original stack of cards. In some casinos, a plastic card is handed to the player to be inserted somewhere in the deck, then the cards on top of the card are placed below it. Either cut is legitimate.

After the cards are cut, the dealer places them all together, and then removes the top card, and either places it on the bottom of the deck, face up (but in such a manner that the players cannot see its value) or takes the top card and places it in a small plastic case to his right, face down. If he does the latter, then all future discards—that is, cards already played out—will be placed atop that card. If he turns the card face up at the bottom of the deck, then all future discards will be placed face up below that burned card.

The above paragraph describes what is meant by **burning a card**. This is a ritual carried out in practically all casinos, and hearkens back to the days when the casino was worried that someone would cut to a precise part of the deck, and thus take advantage of knowledge of the top card. Which still might be done, for all we know.

Making a Bet

As the dealer holds the cards, getting ready to deal, the players make their bets. We will see a rectangular printed box right in front of our seat, and this is where our chips go.

The bet must be made prior to the deal of the cards. It must be at least the minimum allowed at the table, and cannot be more than the maximum permitted at the table.

But we're not thinking of $500 bets (usually the maximum at most casinos) as we put out two $1 chips. We're going to get our feet wet and test the waters that Lady Luck swims in so cunningly. Our chips are now in our betting box, and since the other two players have also made their bets, the dealer is ready to deal out the cards.

The Deal

The first baseman gets the top card, face down, and then the second player gets his card, and we then get ours. The last of the first cards to be dealt goes to the dealer, also face down. Now a second card goes out in the same order, but the dealer turns over this card, his upcard.

We now all have original hands of two cards, and can exercise our various options, or *act upon* our hands. For purposes of this illustration, we're simply going to make a decision as to whether to hit or stand.

Hitting or Standing—How To

To refresh our recollection, hitting means drawing a card to our original hand. We can hit our hand as often as we care to, so long as the total of the cards doesn't exceed 21.

To hit—that is, ask for another card—we pick up our original cards and scrape the edges on the felt surface toward us. This is the universal signal for a hit in all casinos that deal cards face down. The dealer will give you another card from the top of the stock he's holding in his hand.

If we want another card after our original hit, we scrape again. Simple as that. If we're satisfied with our hand, we slide the cards under our bet chips, and don't touch either the cards or the chips again.

As you may have noticed, no verbal commands are given to the dealer. The whole game can be played silently with these signals.

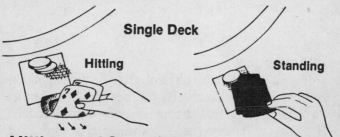

Single Deck

Hitting

Standing

Hitting and Standing in Multiple Deck Games

When all the players' cards are dealt *face up*, which is the usual case in multiple deck games involving four or more decks, there are different signals used by players when they wish to hit or stand.

If a player wants to draw another card, his signal for a hit is to point his index finger at the cards. Another card will be given to him by the dealer. Or the player may scratch the felt surface of the table behind his cards with his index finger, and this is also a signal for a hit. Either signal is universally accepted in American casinos.

If that same player wants to stand with his total, he simply waves his hand over the cards, with the palm face down, and the dealer will respect this signal and pass him by.

Multiple Deck

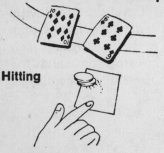

Hitting   Standing

Blackjacks

If a player is fortunate enough to be dealt a black-jack, which is an ace and 10-value card dealt to him as an original hand, he also turns these over immediately. But now for the good news. If the dealer doesn't have a blackjack also, the player will be paid off at once at 3-2, and his cards will be taken out of play.

Dealer's Upcard

In single deck games, if the dealer's upcard is a 10 (or 10-value), he immediately peeks at his hole card (the face down card below the upcard) to see if he has a blackjack. If he does, he turns the ace over and collects bets from all players who themselves don't have blackjacks. If he doesn't have an ace in the hole, he continues dealing the game.

If the dealer has an ace as an upcard, then he will ask the players if they want *insurance.* We'll go into this later.

Playing the Hand

Let's assume, in our theoretical game at the table

with the other two players, that the dealer's upcard is a 9. He doesn't have to peek at his hole card, for there's no way he can have a blackjack with a 9 showing.

The first baseman is the first to act on his hand. Remember, the players act first—that is, hit or stand—and then the dealer acts last, after all the players have made their decisions.

The first baseman scrapes his cards for a hit. He is dealt a queen. He scrapes the cards again for another hit, and gets a 7. Disgustedly, he turns over the cards he has been holding. He had a 3 and a 2, making his original hand a 5; with the queen and 7 he now holds 22, and has busted. The dealer takes away the first baseman's chips and cards and now turns his attention to the second player.

This player scrapes for a hit, gets a 4, and then happily slides his cards under his chips, a signal that he is now standing on his total. The dealer now turns to us. We look at our cards and find we hold a jack and a 9. Our 19 is a strong total, so we stand by—sliding the cards under our chips. Now it's the dealer's turn. He turns over his hole card.

His hole card was a 3, giving him a total of 12. Under the rules of the game, he must hit this hand, since it totals less than 17. He takes a card for himself by putting the top card of the stock face up next to his two original cards. It is a 4, giving him a 16. He must hit again. He has no options. His next card is a king. The dealer has gone over 21 and busted.

At this point, he takes the second player's original cards from under the chips and turns them over. This player had a 10 and a 6 for a 16, and drew the 4, giving him a 20. He is paid off at even-money. We are also paid off at even-money. It really didn't matter what totals either we or the second baseman had at this point, since the dealer busted and automatically lost.

After all the discards are put away, another round of play begins. Again, we all get two cards, and the dealer's upcard this time is a jack. Therefore, he peeks at his hole card, and when he finds he doesn't have a blackjack, he now turns toward the first baseman and the game goes on as before.

After a few rounds of play, even though there are cards left in the stock the dealer is holding, he'll shuffle up the cards. This is done to prevent card counters, experts who keep track of played out cards, from having an advantage over the house by knowing just what cards are left in the stock and betting accordingly.

Multiple Deck Games

By multiple deck games, we are referring to all games which use more than one deck.

When 4 or more decks are used, they're dealt from a **shoe**, a rectangular box which permits the cards to be slid out one at a time.

Double Deck Games

When two decks are used, these are still hand-held and all signals used by players are the same as in a single deck game. There are relatively few double deck games in comparison with either single or four and six deck games.

Splitting Pairs

Doubling Down

5. The Player's Options

Splitting Pairs

A player may split any matching cards of the same rank (pairs) if dealt as an original hand. For example, if he or she is dealt two 8s, these may be split. When pairs are split, they are turned over by the player if dealt face down; or separated, if dealt face up. Then a bet equal to the original bet is placed on the newly split card.

For example, if a player had bet $5, and received two 8s, and split them, then an additional $5 bet will be placed on the separated (split) 8. In essence, the player will now be betting on and playing out two hands.

He draws cards on the first 8 till he is satisfied with that total, and then he draws cards to the second 8, just as though this was an original hand.

Any pairs can be split, and for purposes of pairs, all 10-value cards are considered pairs. For example, a 10 and queen, or a jack and king, are considered pairs, but as we shall see, 10s should not be split.

Aces may be split, but unlike all other pairs, only one additional card will be dealt to each ace. Nevertheless, aces equal 11 and they should always be split.

Doubling Down

A player may double his bet on his original hand, at his option. When he does this, he will receive an additional card, and *one card* only. Therefore, it's important to remember that after doubling down, you can't stand on your original hand's total; you're going to be given an additional card by the dealer.

In practically all casinos except for the Northern Nevada ones, the rules permit doubling down on any two-card total. In Northern Nevada, only 10s and 11s may be doubled down.

When doubling down, a player turns over his cards if dealt face down, and puts out a bet equal to the original bet. When the cards have been dealt face up, he simply puts out an additional bet.

Surrender

In a few casinos, the player is allowed to forfeit half his original bet if he or she doesn't want to play the hand against the dealer. This is called **surrender.**

For example, suppose a player has a big bet out and the dealer shows a 10 as his upcard. The player has been dealt a 16, and feels that if he hits the hand, he'll bust, and if he stands, the dealer will have a 17 or more to beat him anyway. So, in those casinos allowing surrender, this player may surrender his hand. It's one of the few instances in which a verbal statement of the player's intent is made. He says *"Surrender,"* and the dealer will remove his cards and half his bet.

Insurance

When the dealer's upcard is an ace, before he peeks at his hole card the players are given the opportunity to *insure* their bets. The dealer will ask "Insurance?" and the players may bet up to one-half of their original bet that the dealer has a 10-value card in the hole.

If the dealer has a blackjack, the insurance bet wins, and is paid off at 2-1, but the original bet loses, and so, in essence, it's a standoff.

Therefore, an insurance bet is really a wager that the dealer has a blackjack. If he has one, the bet wins. If he doesn't have a 10-value card in the hole, the insurance bet is immediately lost and taken away and the game continues.

For example, if a player had a $10 bet out and then made a $5 insurance bet and the dealer didn't have a blackjack, the $5 bet would be taken away by the dealer. However, the game would now continue and the original $10 bet is still valid.

If the dealer in the above instance had a blackjack, he'd take away the player's original $10 bet and then pay $10, at 2-1 on the $5 insurance bet. In essence, it's a push.

6. Winning Basic Strategies

Now we come to the chapter that will show you how to win at blackjack, using correct basic strategies.

Hitting and Standing Strategy

We'll divide this strategy into hard and soft totals. Remember, a hard hand is anyone that doesn't contain an ace, or where an ace is counted as a 1 and not an 11.

For our considerations, all hard hands will begin with a total of 12. Hands below that total can be hit without worrying about busting.

Whether to hit or stand on any hand depends on two factors: the player's total and the dealer's upcard.

The following table will show the correct hitting and standing basic strategies:

Chart 1
Hitting and Standing—Hard Totals

	2	3	4	5	6	7	8	9	10	A
11 or less	H	H	H	H	H	H	H	H	H	H
12	H	H	S	S	S	H	H	H	H	H
13	S	S	S	S	S	H	H	H	H	H
14	S	S	S	S	S	H	H	H	H	H
15	S	S	S	S	S	H	H	H	H	H
16	S	S	S	S	S	H	H	H	H	H
17-21	S	S	S	S	S	S	S	S	S	S

H = Hit   S = Stand

Whenever the dealer shows a 7 or higher upcard (8, 9, 10 or ace), we assume that he already has a total of 17 and must stand with that total. Of course, that's not always the case, but it happens frequently enough for us to try and improve our total if it's below 17.

That's why we hit all hands from 12 through 16 when the dealer shows a 7, 8, 9, 10 or ace.

When the dealer shows a *bust* or *stiff* card, a 2, 3, 4, 5, or 6, we stand on all totals, except a hard 12 against a dealer's 2 or 3.

The reason we hit a 12 against a dealer's 2 or 3 up-card is that there are relatively fewer cards to bust our (and the dealer's) hand in that situation. Other than a 12 against the 2 and 3, we stand on all other totals when the dealer shows a stiff card. Our strategy in this regard is to force the dealer to hit his stiff hand and bust it, while we still have a valid hand.

It may be hard to memorize the table, but if you play out and practice some hands at home looking at the hitting and standing table, it will become easier to understand. And if you see the reasoning behind it, it's easier still.

Of course, we never hit a hard 17 or higher total, no matter what the dealer shows. The odds are very strong that we'll bust, and if our total is 19 or better we're favored to win by standing.

What we don't want to do is hit stiff totals from 12 to 16 when the dealer shows a 4, 5 or 6. These are the worst cards the dealer can have (and the best for us to see as upcards) because he's most likely to bust his hand with those upcards. And it would be foolish of us to bust first, when the dealer has such a good chance of busting and losing.

Hitting and Standing with Soft Totals

A soft total is any hand that contains an ace which is counted as 11 points. Thus, an ace-6 is a soft 17. There will be two tables here—the first is to be used in all jurisdictions other than Northern Nevada, for only hard 10s and 11s can be doubled down there.

Chart 2
Hitting, Standing or Doubling Down
with Soft Totals

	2	3	4	5	6	7	8	9	10	A
A2-A5	H	H	D	D	D	H	H	H	H	H
A6	D	D	D	D	D	H	H	H	H	H
A7	S	D	D	D	D	S	S	H	H	S
A8	S	S	S	S	S	S	S	S	S	S
A9	S	S	S	S	S	S	S	S	S	S

H = Hit   S = Stand   D = Double

All soft totals of 17 or below should be hit or doubled down. When the dealer shows a 4, 5 or 6 these soft totals will be doubled down.

The ace-6, the soft 17, will *never be stood upon.* It will either be hit, or doubled down. When you see a player standing with a soft 17, you'll know he's very weak, and a loser.

The soft 19 and 20 are very strong and you should be content to stand with these totals. But the soft 18 is the tricky one. It is hit against the dealer's 9 and 10 up-card, and doubled down when the dealer holds the 3 through the 6. Practice these hands, and it will come naturally to you after a while.

The next table is for use only in Northern Nevada or any other jurisdiction where soft doubling down is not permitted.

Chart 3

Hitting and Standing with Soft Totals

	2	3	4	5	6	7	8	9	10	A
A2-A6	H	H	H	H	H	H	H	H	H	H
A7	S	S	S	S	S	S	S	H	H	S
A8-A9	S	S	S	S	S	S	S	S	S	S

H = Hit   S = Stand

As we see from the above table, we *always hit* the soft 17, and hit the soft 18 against the dealer's 9 or 10. These are important rules to remember, as well as standing on soft 19 or 20.

Doubling Down Strategies

The next table shows doubling down strategies, which correctly followed, give the player a tremendous edge over the casino. This table covers only hard doubling down totals, since the soft ones have already been covered in the previous section.

In Northern Nevada, where only a hard 10 or 11 can be doubled down, use the lines showing the 10 and 11.

Chart 4
Doubling Down with Hard Totals

	2	3	4	5	6	7	8	9	10	A
8(5-3, 4-4)				D	D					
9		D	D	D	D					
10	D	D	D	D	D	D	D	D		
11	D	D	D	D	D	D	D	D	D	D

D = Double Down   Blank = Do Not Double Down

From this table we see that we *never* double down with a hard total of less than 8. Be sure to double down when you hold an 11. Many players are afraid to double down against a dealer's 10, but if you get a 10-value card on the 11, you have a 21, and can't lose.

If playing in Atlantic City, or in a casino where the dealer doesn't look at his hole card till all the players have acted upon their hands, the same double down rules apply. If the dealer finds he has a blackjack, the extra double down wager will be returned. The same holds true when splitting pairs. Only the original bet is lost.

Splitting Pairs

As we know, a player has the option of splitting any paired cards from his original hand, such as 3-3, 8-8, 9-9 and so forth. And all 10-value cards are considered pairs, such as jack-king, or 10-queen. The following chart shows correct splitting strategies. Split only those pairs shown on the chart.

Chart 5
Splitting Pairs

	2	3	4	5	6	7	8	9	10	A
22		Spl.	Spl.	Spl.	Spl.	Spl.				
33			Spl.	Spl.	Spl.	Spl.				
66	Spl.	Spl.	Spl.	Spl.	Spl.					
77	Spl.	Spl.	Spl.	Spl.	Spl.	Spl.				
88	Spl.	Spl.	Spl.	Spl.	Spl.	Spl.	Spl.	Spl.	Spl.	Spl.
99	Spl.	Spl.	Spl.	Spl.	Spl.		Spl.	Spl.		
AA	Spl.	Spl.	Spl.	Spl.	Spl.	Spl.	Spl.	Spl.	Spl.	Spl.

Spl. = Split   Blank = Do Not Split

Do not split 44, 55, 10s
Always split 88, AA

Be sure to split 8s and aces. A pair of 8s add up to 16, the worst stiff total a player can have, while 8s separately will form the base for a much stronger hand.

And aces should be split, because each ace adds up to 11, and a 10-value card drawn to that 11 is a powerful 21.

On the other hand, never split 4s and 5s. Two 4s add up to 8, while an individual 4 can end up as a stiff hand and a bad one at that. The 5s together add up to 10, and in most situations will be a doubled down hand. An individual 5 will usually lead to a stiff or a busted hand.

Don't split 10s (any 10-value pairs). These add up to 20, usually a winning hand. Splitting 10s is a bad move, and only the weakest players make it.

Some players will split any pair, no matter what the

dealer's upcard, thinking this is correct. But it isn't, and will end up costing the player money. Stick to our pair splits and you'll come out a winner. They all make sense.

For example, we don't split 7s against an 8 because if the player gets two 10-value cards, one on each 7, he'll still have only 17 and the dealer might already have an 18. And we don't split 9s against a dealer's 7 because two 9s add up to an 18, and the dealer might only have a 17. And we split 9s against the 8 because the 18 might only be a push, whereas a 10-value card on a 9 makes it a winner.

Resplitting Pairs

If an original pair should be split, then subsequent cards of the same rank should also be split. For example, suppose the dealer shows a 6 as his upcard, and you have a pair of 8s. You split the 8s, and get a 5 on the first 8 for a 13. Now you must stand on that hand because the *Hitting and Standing Strategies* call for no further cards to be drawn.

On the second 8, you're dealt another 8. This should be split and another bet put out. The rule is: resplit pairs where the first split is correct. Not all casinos allow resplitting. For example, aces generally can't be resplit. All other pairs can be resplit in practically all casinos except in Atlantic City.

Insurance

Whenever the dealer shows an ace as his upcard, he'll ask if any player wants insurance. As explained before, the insurance bet is a bet that the dealer *has* a

10-value card in the hole and thus has a blackjack.

In most cases, it's a bad bet. Don't take insurance unless you're familiar with an advanced card counting system.

Surrender

This is allowed in some casinos, where a player may forfeit half his bet and decide not to play his or her original hand against the dealer.

When you have the chance to surrender, stick to the following rules: surrender 15s and 16s against a dealer's 10, and a 16 against a dealer's ace. (Do not surrender 8-8—split it.)

Otherwise, don't surrender.

Chart 6
Master Strategy Chart

	2	3	4	5	6	7	8	9	10	A
7 or less	H	H	H	H	H	H	H	H	H	H
62	H	H	H	H	H	H	H	H	H	H
44, 53	H	H	H	D	D	H	H	H	H	H
9	D	D	D	D	D	H	H	H	H	H
10	D	D	D	D	D	D	D	D	H	H
11	D	D	D	D	D	D	D	D	D	D
12	H	H	S	S	S	H	H	H	H	H
13	S	S	S	S	S	H	H	H	H	H
14	S	S	S	S	S	H	H	H	H	H
15	S	S	S	S	S	H	H	H	H	H
16	S	S	S	S	S	H	H	H	H	H
A2	H	H	D*	D*	D*	H	H	H	H	H
A3	H	H	D*	D*	D*	H	H	H	H	H
A4	H	H	D*	D*	D*	H	H	H	H	H
A5	H	H	D*	D*	D*	H	H	H	H	H
A6	D*	D*	D*	D*	D*	H	H	H	H	H
A7	S	D*	D*	D*	D*	S	S	H	H	S
A8	S	S	S	S	S	S	S	S	S	S
A9	S	S	S	S	S	S	S	S	S	S
22	H	Spl.	Spl.	Spl.	Spl.	Spl.	H	H	H	H
33	H	H	Spl.	Spl.	Spl.	Spl.	H	H	H	H
66	Spl.	Spl.	Spl.	Spl.	Spl.	H	H	H	H	H
77	Spl.	Spl.	Spl.	Spl.	Spl.	Spl.	H	H	H	H
88	Spl.	Spl.	Spl.	Spl.	Spl.	Spl.	Spl.	Spl.	Spl.	Spl.
99	Spl.	Spl.	Spl.	Spl.	Spl.	S	Spl.	Spl.	S	S
AA	Spl.	Spl.	Spl.	Spl.	Spl.	Spl.	Spl.	Spl.	Spl.	Spl.

H = Hit   S = Stand   D = Double   Spl. = Split

*Where soft doubling not permitted, as in Northern Nevada, hit (do not double).

7. Card Counting and Money Management
Card Counting

Card counting, or keeping track of the cards already played out, is used by experts to beat the casino, and many of these experts have been barred from play.

This guidebook is not going to deal with card counting, other than to state that when a high proportion of 10-value cards and aces have been dealt out, the deck is unfavorable for the player. On the other hand, many smaller cards, such as 2s, 3s, 4s, 5s, 6s and 7s have been dealt out, the deck or decks are favorable for the player.

By watching the game closely, a player can get a good idea of the cards already dealt. For example, if on the first round of play in a single deck game, a disproportionate number of aces and 10s were dealt, then the deck is unfavorable. If a whole group of smaller cards showed on the opening round, with few aces or tens, then the deck is favorable.

A good rule in a single deck game only is to raise the bet when the first round showed a high proportion of small cards dealt out, and to lower the bet when this round showed a higher proportion of tens and aces.

With each round that follows, you see that cumulatively, more tens than normal have been dealt, keep your bet low. On the other hand, when you notice more small cards have been played out, raise your bet. This strategy works because a single deck is sensitive to changes in deck composition.

To effectively beat the casinos, whether playing a single or multiple deck game, we highly recommend that you learn a card counting strategy.

See back page for information on the GRI Pro-Count; the most effective card counting strategy ever produced for the average player. It is simple to learn yet extremely powerful. It will give any reader of this book a winning edge over the casino with just a few hours practice at home.

Money Management

Blackjack games can be like rollercoasters, with large winning and losing swings during the course of play. Be prepared and don't get discouraged by these swings, because correct play will make you a winner in the long run.

As a rule of thumb, multiply your normal bet by 40 to determine how much to put on the table for one session of play. If you're betting $2 at a time, $80 will be sufficient. With $5 bets, about $200 will be needed. You can even hedge and take less, about $50 for $2 bets and $100 for $5 bets, but that's cutting it a little too thin.

Remember, play only with money you can afford to lose, that won't affect you financially and/or emotionally. Try to double your stake at the table. If you do, leave at once. You've done well. Or, if the table is choppy, and you're ahead, endeavor to leave a winner.

If you're losing, don't lose more than you bring to the table. Set a loss limit, and never reach into your pocket for more money. The first loss is the cheapest.

Money management can be as important as good play. Keep control of your emotions and your money, and you'll be a winner.

8. Glossary of Blackjack Terms

Anchorman—Also called **Third Baseman**. The player in the last seat or the player who acts upon his hand last at the table.

Blackjack—1. The name of the casino game; also known as "21." 2. An original hand consisting of an ace and 10-value card, paid off at 3-2 if held by a player.

Burning a Card—The removal of the top card by the dealer before dealing out cards on the first round of play.

Busting—Also known as **Breaking**. Drawing cards to a hand so that its total is 22 or more, a loser.

Card Counting—Keeping mental track of the cards played out to see if the deck is favorable or unfavorable.

Chips—The gambling tokens issued by the casino to take the place of cash, for betting purposes.

Dealer—The casino employee in charge of the blackjack game, who deals out cards and collects and pays off bets.

Deck—The standard pack of cards containing 52 cards of four suits.

Double Down—The doubling of an original bet by a player, who will then receive only one additional card.

Draw—See **Hit.**

Favorable Deck—A deck whose remaining cards are to the advantage of the player as far as probability of winning is concerned.

First Baseman—The player who receives cards and acts upon them first. Usually occupies the first end seat at the table.

Hand—The cards the players hold and act upon.

Hard Total—A hand containing no aces, or where the ace is counted as 1.

Hit—Also called **Draw.** The act of getting one or more cards for the original hand.

Hole Card—The unseen dealer's card.

Insurance—A bet that can be made when a dealer shows an ace as an upcard. This bet wins if the dealer has a blackjack.

Multiple Deck—The use of more than one deck in the game of casino blackjack.

Natural—A term for a blackjack.

Push—A tie between the dealer and player, where no money changes hands. It's a standoff.

Round of Play—A complete cycle of play where all the players and the dealer act upon their hands.

Shoe—A device used when dealing four or more decks.

Shuffle, Shuffle Up—The mixing up of the cards by the dealer.

Single Deck Game—A game in hich only one deck of cards is used.

Soft Total—A hand containing an ace that counts as 11 points. Example, an ace-9 is a soft 20 total.

Splitting Pairs—The separation of two cards of equal rank, such as 8s, so that they're played as two separate hands.

Standing, Standing Pat—Not hitting a hand.

Stiff Hand—Any hand that may bust if drawn to, such as a hard 12-16.

Ten-Value Card—The 10, jack, queen or king, all valued at ten points.

Third Baseman—See **Anchorman**.

Tip or Toke—A gratuity given to or bet for the dealer by a player.

Twenty-One—Another name for the casino game of blackjack.

Upcard—The open card of the dealer which can be seen by the players prior to their acting on their hands.

Three. Craps

9. Introduction

Craps is certainly the most exciting and the fastest of all casino games. There is action, if the player wishes, on every roll of the dice. It's also a game in which one can let loose; it doesn't matter how excited you get at the table, or how you show your emotions. This not only makes the game exciting, but fun as well. However, it's a casino game, after all, and money can be won or lost while playing it. This book will show you how to play the game correctly, how to make the best bets and how to come out a winner if lady luck is on your side.

Each aspect of the game is gone into, so that even the novice, or person unfamiliar with craps will know all that is necessary to play the game intelligently and avoid the worst bets, the ones that favor the house with too much of an edge.

So, good luck. Following the advice outlined in this book will give you the best chance of winning at this most exciting of games.

10. Understanding the Dice

The game of casino craps is played with two dice and each die has six numbered sides.

The numbers are in the form of dots, running from one to six. Thus, with two dice in play, the lowest number that can be rolled is 2; made up of the one spot coming up on each die. The highest number is 12, which is made up of six spots coming up on each die. With two dice in operation, there are thirty-six possible combinations that can be rolled, with the numbers from two to twelve as possibilities.

Casino dice are built to exacting standards, so that there is little chance of certain numbers showing up more often than others because of faulty design or manufacture. They're approximately 3/4 of an inch measured on each side, and are made as close to exact cubes as modern machinery will allow.

When you're playing the game, and it's your turn to roll the dice, if you look closely, you'll see imprinted on the dice two other things besides the dots representing the numbers. First of all, the name of the casino, or its logo will be shown. Secondly, there'll be a code number. Individual sets of dice are made for particular casinos, often coming in a particular color, such as green or red, the most common in American gambling casinos. In addition, code numbers are put on the dice so that cheats can't substitute other dice for the ones regularly used. This safeguards both the casino and the players in the course of a game.

Dice Combinations

The next table shows all the possible combinations of two rolled dice.

The above table is symmetrical in size, with the 7 standing firmly in the center and all other numbers sliding away from it. The 7 can be rolled no matter what number shows up on one die; it is unique in that aspect. For example, a 6 cannot be rolled if a six shows on one die, and an 8 can't be rolled if a 1 shows up on any die.

The seven is the most important number by far in the game of casino craps, and determines all the odds.

Chart 1
Dice Combinations

Number	Combinations	Ways to Roll
2	1-1	One
3	1-2, 2-1	Two
4	1-3, 3-1, 2-2	Three
5	1-4, 4-1, 2-3, 3-2	Four
6	1-5, 5-1, 2-4, 4-2, 3-3	Five
7	1-6, 6-1, 2-5, 5-2, 3-4, 4-3	Six
8	2-6, 6-2, 3-5, 5-3, 4-4	Five
9	3-6, 6-3, 4-5, 5-4	Four
10	4-6, 6-4, 5-5	Three
11	5-6, 6-5	Two
12	6-6	One

Correct Odds, House Payoff and Edge

The **house advantage** or **edge** is the difference between the player's chances of winning the bet, called the **correct odds**, and the casino's actual payoff, called the **house payoff** or simply, the **payoff**. For example, the correct odds of rolling a 7 are 5 to 1. Since the house will payoff only 4 to 1 should the 7 be thrown, they maintain an edge of 16.67 percent on this wager.

BEAT THE ODDS

Nevada Craps Layout

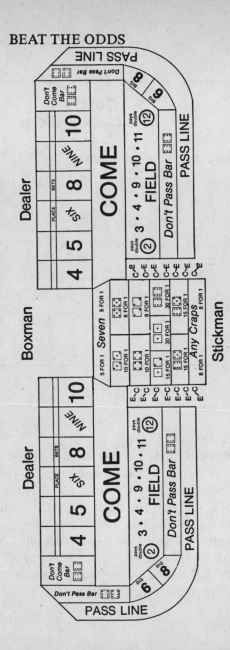

11. The Table and Layout

The Table

The average craps table is about the size of a large billiards table and is built to accomodate anywhere from twelve to twenty-four players. There is a felt covered surface known as the **layout**, around which are walls which form the table, and on which are rails to hold the players' chips.

The main purpose of the layout is to give the players what they're at the casino for, action. They have a chance to make a variety of bets, all of which are favorable to the house, that is, the odds on each bet favor the house.

We can see that there are essentially three sections on the layout. There are two identical side areas separated by a center area. The center area is where all the center, or proposition bets are made. As we shall see, none of the bets in this section are worth a red penny; they're all bad, that is, highly unfavorable to the player. The following is the center layout.

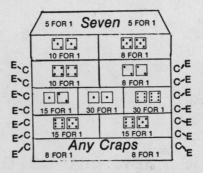

The two side areas are identical and they contain the best wagers for the player to make, since they give the house the smallest advantage over the gamblers. This is the best area to put your money.

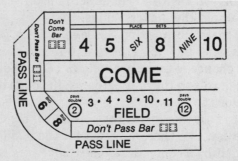

12. Casino Personnel

The Crew of Dealers

A casino craps crew is made up of four individuals, but only three work the table at one time, with the fourth **on break**, that is, taking a rest from his chores. The crew usually is made up of men, though more and more women are seen as integral parts of craps crews.

The men and women who make up the working crew do not have set jobs at the table. They move around from position to position. This rotation keeps them alert and adds flavor to the game, for each dealer has a different personality and an upbeat dealer or crew can make a game come alive.

The Stickman

One of the dealers faces the other two. He or she is known as the **stickman**, or is said to be **on the stick.**

This is because he or she holds a malleable stick in his hand, which is used first of all, to push the dice to a new shooter, then to gather in dice that have been thrown and to hold them with the stick till all payoffs and collections have been made by the other dealers.

The stickman also is in charge of all the center or **proposition** bets, which are under his direct control. He collects losing bets and pushes them to the boxman, whom we will discuss later. The stickman directs the other dealers to pay off winning bets that occur on the center of the table.

If a player makes a propostion or center bet, the chips are thrown to the stickman to be put in the correct betting box. But the stickman doesn't pay off bets, and has no direct contact with the players except for pushing the dice toward the shooter with his stick.

The dealer on the stick has one other important duty. He calls the game. If a new shooter is to be selected, he announces *"new shooter coming out."* If there is a come-out roll, he announces that as well. After the dice are thrown, he calls the number thrown, such as *"five"*. He may also add, *"five, no field,"* to indicate that it is not paid off on the field bets.

Often the personality of the stickman infuses the craps game and determines whether it will be lively or dull.

Dealers On-Base

These are the two standing dealers who face the stickman, and each covers an end area of the layout. They have direct contact with the players. They make change, **change color** (change chips for others of different denominations), pay off winning bets and collect losing ones.

They also handle the players' chips when they want to make center bets or bets they can't reach, such as odds bets on don't come and come points.

These dealers are said to be **on base**. When you first come to a table, it will be a dealer on base that you'll give your cash to. He'll give you the correct casino chips as soon as the sum is verified by the boxman.

The standing dealer will also answer any questions you might have as to the table limits, how much you can wager on any particular bet and whether or not single or double odds are permitted at the table.

Each standing dealer has a **marker puck,** a black and white round plastic disk, which is on the black side in the corner don't come box prior to a come-out roll. This disk is turned up to its white side and put into a point number box after a point is established on the *"come-out roll"*. A come-out roll will be explained later.

First and foremost, the dealer is there to help you, the player, to make certain your bets have been correctly made and to answer any of your questions about the game.

The Boxman

The crew of dealers wear the house uniform, but the boxman is usually dressed in a jacket or suit. He is in charge of the game, and sits between the two on-base dealers, facing the stickman.

The boxman supervises the game, makes sure that the payoffs are correct, makes certain that the cash given to the dealer is verified, and in short, he sits there protecting the casino's bankroll, for most of the chips on the table are right in front of him, under his domain and protection.

If the dice are thrown off the table, they must first be returned to the boxman, who examines the die or dice to make sure they haven't been tampered with and are the same die or dice that were thrown, and not new dice inserted in the game by cheats. To do this, he looks for both the casino logo and the coded number on all casino dice.

If there's a dispute between a player and a dealer, as sometimes happens, the boxman has the final word. Generally, he will side with the player, unless it is a flagrant objection by the player, but thereafter, in further disputes, he'll not give the player the benefit of the doubt.

Casino Executives

Since craps table revenue is an important aspect of the profits of a casino, not only are the crew of dealers and boxman involved with the game, but behind the table, in the *craps pit* are several other casino employees, executives of the house. These might include a **floorman**, who supervises a couple of tables, and is there in case any of the players want to get credit. And above him, in charge of all the craps tables in what is known as the craps pit, is the **pitboss**, the final authority on credit and disputes.

Tipping

Tipping, or **toking** as it is called in the casinos, is a voluntary practice. Only the crew of dealers are tipped, not the boxman or the casino executives. If a player is winning a lot and feels in a buoyant mood, or he has received good services from the dealers, then he may tip them. The usual practice is to make a bet for *the boys* by throwing a chip toward the center or proposition bets, and making one of those high yielding but poor odds bets. Just say *"for the boys"*. The crew will understand that this bet is for them, and should thank you for it. They appreciate tokes because that's the main source of their income.

13. How to Play Craps

In this section we're going to study just how to play craps, and show the essential game, what's involved and so forth. So let's imagine that we know nothing about the game, and we're in a gambling casino, approaching a craps table. There are a few open spots around the rails and we move into one of them.

The first thing we want to do is make a bet; but before we can do that, we should change our cash into casino chips, or **checks** as the professionals call them. We can play with cash, make bets in cash all night long, but the casino discourages this, for it's cumbersome and slows the game down, and has to be counted and recounted. Chips are easier, fit into betting areas better, and can be paid off more easily. In fact, even if you wager in cash, you'll be paid off with chips.

Casino Chips

Chips usually come in standard denominations of $1, $5, $25 and $100. Some casinos have $500 or larger denomination chips and others have smaller denominations, down to 25¢ chips. But for purposes of this book we're going to stick with the $1 to $100 chips.

All right, we're at the table, and we take some cash out of our pocket. We're going to gamble with $200 worth. This cash is given to the standing dealer nearest us, and the cash will go over to the seated boxman who'll count and verify its amount. Once it's verified, he'll tell the dealer to give you $200 in chips, while the cash is pushed down with a paddle into a slot on the table, to fall into a **drop box.**

Now the casino has our cash, but we have its chips. The dealer will ask what denominations we want. We might ask for a stack of twenty $5 chips and four $25 chips. Long-time gamblers refer to $5 chips as **nickels** and $25 chips as **quarters.** The dealer will hand you twenty $5 chips and four $25 chips and now you're ready to make a bet.

The Shooter

When you arrive at the table, someone will be ready to throw the dice. This is the **shooter.** Whatever he throws is what determines whether bets are won or lost.

Let's assume that a new shooter is about to be given the dice. Each player gets a turn at being a shooter. The dice go around the table in a clockwise manner. Anyone who's selected as the shooter may pass up the chance; there's no stigma attached to not being a shooter. If the dice are refused, then the next person, to that player's left, will be offered the dice.

The shooter will be given from six to eight dice, of which he'll select only two. He will generally roll with these same dice for his entire shoot; through sometimes eccentric players will change the dice or if one is rolled off the table or temporarily lost, another one will replace the lost die.

But this decision rests solely with the shooter. Other players at the table can't demand that the dice be changed. While a person is a shooter, he or she is the center of attention.

14. The Line and Free-Odds Bets

Making A Bet

Before the shooter rolls the dice for the first time, or after he has made his point (which will be explained later) there is a *come-out* roll. Prior to the come-out roll, most of the players at the table bet either for or against the dice by making either a pass-line or don't pass bet. This is done by putting a chip or chips into the appropriate areas on the layout. By far the most popular bet in casino craps is the pass-line wager.

Pass-Line Wager and Come-Out Roll

The area that accomodates the pass-line bet runs the full length of each side area, to give the bettors easy access to this wager.

PASS LINE

This bet can only be made prior to the opening roll of the dice, the come-out roll. A come-out roll can easily be ascertained, for there is a round disk that is black and white and when it is resting on its black side in the corner of the numbered boxes, in the don't come box, then there is a come-out roll about to commence.

When this same disk is on its white side and in one of the numbered boxes on the layout, in the 4, 5, 6, 8, 9 or 10 box, then that is the point established by the come-out roll, and no more line bets are permitted. A **line bet** is either a pass-line or don't pass wager.

The come-out roll is the most important throw in craps. It determines either immediate wins or losses, or what point is established.

The bettor wagering on the pass-line wants the dice to win, or pass. He is known as the **right** bettor, and wins immediately at even-money if:

A 7 or 11 is rolled on the come-out.

He loses immediately if:

A 2, 3 or 12, all known as **craps** is rolled on the come-out.

When a shooter rolls a 2, 3 or 12, he is said to have

crapped out, but he doesn't lose his shoot. After all pass-line bets are collected, and all don't pass bets paid off, he continues his shoot.

If the come-out roll is a 4, 5, 6, 8, 9 or 10, that number is the **point**, and must be repeated before a 7 is thrown for the pass-line bet to win. All other numbers are immaterial to this result, once a point has been established on the come-out. For example, if the point is 4, and subsequently an 11, 12, 3, 2, 8, 8, 9 and 4 is rolled, the pass-line bet is won, because the 4 repeated before a 7 was thrown. None of the other numbers rolled mattered as to this result.

Don't Pass Bet

A player betting **don't pass** is betting against the dice, wagering that they don't pass, or win. He is known as a **wrong** bettor, and he places his chip or chips in the smaller area reserved for don't pass.

A don't pass bettor wins immediately at even-money if:
A 2 or 3 is rolled on the come-out.

He loses immediately if:
A 7 or 11 is rolled.

Don't Pass Bar ⚃⚂

If a 12 is rolled, there's a standoff, and he neither wins nor loses. In some gambling jurisdictions the 2 is substituted for the 12, with the same effect. The 12 or 2 is **barred**, permitting the casino to keep its edge on don't pass wagers.

If a point number is established, the don't pass bettor wins if a 7 comes up before the point is repeated. He'll lose if the point is repeated before a seven comes up again.   The house edge on all line bets, whether they be pass-line or don't pass, is 1.4%. When a player makes these bets, he is giving the house or casino a theoretical win expectation of $1.40 for each $100 bet. However, he can reduce this house edge substantially by making another bet at the same time he makes the line bet. This additional wager is not shown on the layout, but is permissable, and all intelligent craps players should make it. It's known as the **free-odds** bet.

The Free-Odds Bet

This bet can only be made *after* a point number has been established on the come-out. It's made by putting additional chips behind the original bet for pass-line bettors. If won, this additional wager will be paid off at true and correct odds, giving the casino no advantage whatsoever on the wager. That's why it's known as a free-odds bet. If the point is a 4 or 10, the free-odds bet will be paid off at 2-1; a 5 or 9 will be paid off at 3-2, and a 6 or 8 will be paid off at 6-5.

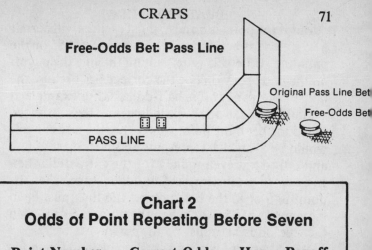

Free-Odds Bet: Pass Line

Original Pass Line Bet

Free-Odds Bet

PASS LINE

Chart 2
Odds of Point Repeating Before Seven

Point Number	Correct Odds	House Payoff
4 or 10	2 to 1	2 to 1
5 or 9	3 to 2	3 to 2
6 or 8	6 to 5	6 to 5

In most casinos the player is limited to a free-odds bet equal to his original pass-line bet. In those casinos the bet is then called a **single odds** bet. But the good news is that, even if one is limited to single odds, a bettor can wager a little more behind the line in certain instances.

For example, if a player bet $5 on the pass-line and the point is 5 or 9, then he's permitted to wager $6 as a free odds bet because the payoff is 3-2, and most casinos won't pay off in half-dollar increments.

When the point is 4 or 10, no matter what is bet the same amount must be wagered as a free odds bet since the payoff is 2-1.

But if the point is 6 and 8, most casinos will permit a $5 free odds bet if the player bets at least $3 on the pass-line. Unless $5 is bet behind the line the payoff on the odds bet won't be the correct 6-5, because the house doesn't pay off in half-dollars. For example, if a gambler bet $6 on the pass-line, and then $6 on the free odds bet if the point was 8, the free odds payoff would be $7, which represents $6 for the first $5 bet, and only $1 at even-money for the extra dollar bet. In order to get the correct free odds return, when the point is 6 or 8, the bets behind the line must be in increments of $5. And when the point is 5 or 9, then the free odds bet must be in increments of $2.

What happens when a pass-line bet and free-odds bet win? What's the payoff? Let's assume a player bets $10 on the pass-line and a point is established. He or she then puts $10 behind the line as a free-odds bet. Here are the payoffs:

Chart 3
Single Odds Payoffs: Right Bettors

Point	Pass-Line Payoff	Free-Odds Payoff	Total
4 or 10	$10	$20 (2-1)	$30
5 or 9	$10	$15 (3-2)	$25
6 or 8	$10	$12 (6-5)	$22

If the 7 comes up before the point is repeated, then the player loses both the pass-line and free odds bets.

When making a free-odds bet, the player reduces the overall house edge from 1.4% to 0.8%, a substantial reduction.

In some casinos, players are permitted to make **double odds** bets. In these casinos, the bettor can place *twice his original bet* behind the line as a free-odds bet. Thus, if he bet $10 on the pass-line, he can put $20 behind the line at correct payoffs. Here's what these payoffs would look like with a $10 pass-line and $20 free odds bet.

Chart 4
Double Odds Payoffs: Right Bettors

Point Payoff	Pass-Line Payoff	Free-Odds Payoff	Total Payoff
4 or 10	$10	$40 (2-1)	$50
5 or 9	$10	$30 (3-2)	$40
6 or 8	$10	$24 (6-5)	$34

A double free-odds bet reduces the house edge down to 0.6%.

Free-odds wagers can be made at any time after a point is established, and can be removed at the player's option at any time prior to a seven-out or the point being repeated. But since it's to the advantage of a player to make a free-odds bet, he or she should always make it, and it should never be removed.

Don't Pass—Laying Free-Odds

A gambler who bets don't pass, betting that the dice will not pass, that the 7 will come up before the point is repeated, can also make free-odds bets. But whereas the pass-line bettor is taking odds, the don't pass bettor is **laying odds**. By making this advantageous bet, the player reduces the casino's overall edge from 1.4% to 0.8%.

Free-Odds Bet: Don't Pass

free-odds bet

original don't pass bet

Don't Pass Bar

Chart 5
Odds of Rolling Seven Before Point Repeats

Point Number	Correct Odds	House Payoff
4 or 10	1 to 2	1 to 2
5 or 9	2 to 3	2 to 3
6 or 8	5 to 6	5 to 6

For example, if a don't pass bettor had put down $10 in the don't pass area and the come-out roll was a 5, then 5 is the point. Now this same don't pass gambler can bet $15 as a free odds bet. What he is doing is betting $15 to win $10, since he is laying 3-2 against the 5 being made. Should the shooter seven-out and not repeat the point, then the don't pass player would win $10 for his don't pass bet and an additional $10 for his free odds bet.

When single odds are permitted, they are determined by the *payoff* amount, not the amount that can be laid against the point. Thus, if the line bet is $10 and the point is 4 or 10, a $20 free odds bet laid against these points will yield a payoff of $10. Likewise $15 against a 5 or 9 will give a payoff of $10, and with a 6 or 8 as a point, the payoff will be $10 if $12 is laid against these points. The following table will show the payoffs if $10 is bet on don't pass and single odds are laid against the various points.

Chart 6
Single Odds Payoffs: Wrong Bettors

Point	Don't Pass Payoff	Free-Odds Payoff	Total Payoff
4 or 10	$10	$10 ($20-$10)	$20
5 or 9	$10	$10 ($15-$10)	$20
6 or 8	$10	$10 ($12-$10)	$20

Like other free-odds bets, these may be laid or taken off at any time after a point is established, at the option of the player.

Some casinos allow double odds bets, and in those houses, a player may lay double the amount he can in a single odds casino. Again, the payoff, not the amount of the odds bet determines how much may be laid.

Thus, a gambler betting $10 as a don't pass bet can lay $40 ($40-$20) if the point is 4 or 10, $30 ($30-$20) if the point is 5 or 9, and $24 ($24-$20) if the point is 6 or 8.

When double odds are laid, the house edge is reduced to 0.6%.

Of course, if the point is made, the don't pass player loses both his original don't pass bet and the double odds free bet.

15. Come and Don't Come Bets

These bets are a little difficult for most players to figure out, but in essence, they're really not hard to understand. And they offer the best odds on the table, along with the line bets, so a craps player should be conversant with them and use them to advantage.

Come Bets

A large section of the layout is devoted to come bets.

COME

This bet is the same as a pass-line bet, except that it can only be made *after* the come-out roll. That's the only difference, really. Let's assume that on the come-out roll, the number thrown was a 9. That's the point. Now, any player can make a come bet.

The come bet is made by putting a chip or chips into the come box. On the very next roll of the dice, if the number is 7 or 11, the come bet wins at even-money. If it's a 2, 3 or 12, the come bet loses immediately. If any other number is rolled, a 4, 5, 6, 8, 9 or 10, then that's the come point. The chips are moved by the dealer to the appropriate number box, which also house the place bets (discussed later).

The player may make a free-odds bet on the come point just as he could on the pass-line point. If its single odds, then a bet equal to the come bet will be given to the dealer and the dealer should be told "odds". He'll place the chip or chips at a slight tilt on the come bet in the appropriate box number. If it's double odds at this casino then a bet double the original come bet can be handed to the dealer as an odds bet.

Let's assume, after the come-out roll of 9, that the next number is 10, and a player had bet $5 on the come. This $5 is moved to box 10, and the player gives the dealer an additional $5 as a free-odds bet. Now, as to the come bet, all that he's concerned with is whether a 10 repeats before the 7. All other numbers are immaterial to the outcome of this bet. If a 10 repeats, the player will be paid $5 for the come bet, and $10 for the free-odds bet at 2-1.

If a 7 comes up before the 10 repeats, then the

player loses both the come and free-odds bets.

Let's assume that instead of a 10 being thrown on the first roll after the come-out, a 7 was rolled. This is an immediate winner for the come bet even though it loses the pass-line bet. Each come roll must be treated as a bet separate from a pass-line wager.

Now, after that 7 is rolled, a player can't make another come bet because there's a new come-out roll, and come bets can only be made after a come-out roll, not at the same time.

The only difference other than timing between a pass-line and come bet is that, if a 7 is thrown on the come-out roll and the player has one or more come bets working, he loses the underlying come bets (because a 7 came up before these number were repeated) but doesn't lose the free-odds bets.

On the come-out roll, the free-odds bets on come wagers aren't *working*. That is, they're **off.** Thus if a player had come bets of $10 each on the 5 and 6, for instance, and also had $10 free-odds on each of those come points, and a 7 is rolled on the come-out roll, he'd lose only $20 on the underlying bets and the $20 in free-odds bets would be returned to him.

Conversely, if either the 5 or 6 had been thrown on the come-out roll, the player would be paid only $10 for the number repeating, and wouldn't get the additional odds bet as a winner. It would simply be returned to him.

Why make come bets? Well, they give the house the same low percentage that it gets on pass-line bets, and enables the player to make a whole series of consecutive wagers at good odds, so that, if the dice get *hot* and a lot of numbers are rolled before a 7 comes up, he can really make a lot of money in a short period of time. But he must remember that when that 7 shows, all the come bets are lost, erased from the table.

Don't Come Bets

The don't come box is much smaller than the come box on the layout, usually tucked in at the end of the place number boxes.

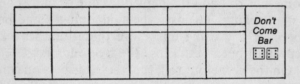

There is usually not that much action on don't come, but that doesn't mean it isn't a valid bet. It's the same as a don't pass bet except for timing, and after the bet is made a player can lay odds against the number just as he or she can on a don't pass bet. The house edge is the same as a don't pass bet, 0.8% when single odds are laid and 0.6% when double odds are laid.

After a come point is rolled, the chip or chips will be taken from the don't come box by the dealer and placed in the area above the numbered box of that come point. Now, the player must give the dealer additional chips to lay odds against the number repeating.

On a don't come bet, if a 7 or 11 is rolled, it's an immediate loser for the don't come player. If a 2 or 3 is rolled, it's an immediate winner at even-money, and if a 12 is rolled, it's a standoff. The same as don't pass in all respects except for timing.

Unlike come bets, don't come bets and odds are always working, even on the come-out roll, so that the player's underlying don't come bet and odds bets are always at risk. On the other hand, if a 7 comes up on the come-out roll, then all the don't come bets are winners, including the free-odds bets laid against the numbers.

Why make don't come bets? The player is hoping for a cold run of dice, where no numbers are repeated. So, after several don't come bets are established, he hopes a 7 comes up and wins all the bets for him. Of course, if a lot of numbers repeat, then he'll be losing those same bets. But the house edge is very small and on a cold table, it's a good way to make money fast.

Free-Odds Bet: Come & Don't Come

Dealer will place free-odds bet atop original bet but offset to distinguish from come or don't come bet.

don't come and free-odds bet

8

NINE

10

come and free-odds bet

16. Place Numbers and Place Bets

The area where place bets can be made is rather large, for not only do place bets get a lot of action, but the same area holds the come and don't come bets.

		PLACE	BETS		
4	5	SIX	8	NINE	10

Place bets can be made on one or more of the numbers that are point numbers; 4, 5, 6, 8, 9 and 10. A place bet can be made at any time, even prior to a come-out roll, but place bets are off and not working on the come-out roll, unless the player wishes them to be working and so instructs the dealer.

The place bets can be made in any denomination up to the house limit, which is generally $500 on all numbers but the 6 and 8, which have $600 limits. They should be made in increments of $5 for all numbers but the 6 and 8, which are in increments of $6, because of the payoffs. Like come bets, they're favored by players betting *right* or with the dice, and like come bets, they allow action on every roll of the dice. But unlike come bets, a place bet doesn't have to repeat twice to get paid off. Once it's made it gets paid off if that number is rolled.

The gambler, to get this kind of action, pays a price. And the price is the house edge, which is much higher than the casino advantage on come bets.

Chart 7
Odds on Place Numbers

Place Number	Casino Payoff	Correct Odds	Casino Edge
4 and 10	9-5	2-1	6.67%
5 and 9	7-5	3-2	4.0%
6 and 8	7-6	6-5	1.52%

As we can easily see, the only possible worthwhile place bet is on the 6 and 8; otherwise the house edge is just too much.

Not only can place bets be made at any time, but they can be raised, lowered or removed at the player's option at any time, as well. Just hand chips to the dealer or instruct him to remove your chips.

Why make place bets? There's really no reason to do so, unless betting on the 6 and 8. If there's a long hot roll, with many numbers repeating, the payoffs can be tremendous. But the house edge is also horrendous, and will eat up the bankroll before a player reaps the benefit of these long rolls.

Buying the 4 and 10

The house edge on the 4 and 10 can be reduced to 4.73% by **buying** either or both numbers. You make this bet by instructing the dealer that you are *"buying"* the 4 or 10 or both numbers, and then handing him the correct number of chips. A buy button will then be put on those chips. The payoff will be 2-1, but each time you get paid off, you pay the equivalent of a 5% commission. In most casinos this commission must be paid at the time the numbers are bought.

Either buying or placing the 4 and 10 is not recommended because of the large house edge.

Lay Wagers

Players who bet against the dice can **lay** bets against any of the point numbers, by so instructing the dealers that they are *laying* against one or more of these numbers. A 5% commission must be paid at this time. This gives the casino the following edges:

Chart 8
House Edge on Lay Wager

Number	Casino Edge
4 and 10	2.44%
5 and 9	3.23%
6 and 8	4.0%

Like place bets, chips are given to the dealer and these bets can be made at any time, in any combinations, or reduced or taken off at any time.

17.   Other Bets

Field Bets

These bets are the favorite of beginning or ignorant players, because they're easy to make, can be made at any time on any roll of the dice, and are paid off or lost immediately. But there's a price to pay, and that's a high casino edge.

The Field Bet takes up a prominent place on the casino layout.

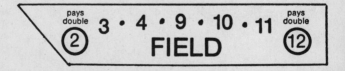

All those numbers look inviting. If a 2 or 12 is thrown, it pays at 2-1. All the other numbers, 3, 4, 9, 10 and 11 pay off at even-money. When the 2 and 12 pay off at 2-1, the house edge on a field bet is 5.5%.

When either the 2 or 12 is paid off at 3-1, then the house edge drops off to 2.70%. This is the case in Atlantic City, Northern Nevada and Downtown Las Vegas. On the Strip, the house edge is 5.5%.

In either case, it's not the best kind of bet to make. The numbers that are missing, the 5, 6, 7 and 8 come up more ways than the numbers on the field bet layout, and though it's a simple bet to make, that's not the reason one should make a field bet.

Why should one make a field bet? There's really no reason to. Avoid it.

Big Six and Big Eight

This bet is prominently displayed, but only small timers make it, putting down a dollar or two and hoping that the 6 or 8 will come up before the 7 is rolled, so that they can collect their even-money winnings.

But there are only five ways to make either a 6 or 8, and six ways to roll a 7, so that the true odds against making the 6 or 8 is 6-5, and when the casino pays off at even-money, it has a 9.09% edge. This bet should never be made except in Atlantic City casinos which will pay off the Big 6 and Big 8 at 7-6, the same as a 6 or 8 place bet, if the bettor puts at least $6 or increments of $6 in the Big 6 or Big 8 box. Otherwise avoid this bet.

Proposition or Center Bets

These bets take up the whole center of the layout and are under the control of the stickman. None of these bets should ever be made, since the house edge is horrendous.

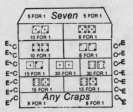

Though the stickman will physically handle the placing and removing of bets in this area, it is with the dealer that the player will generally make his bets and receive his payoffs.

The center bets may be divided into one-roll and other proposition bets.

One Roll Bets

A One-Roll wager wins or loses depending on the very next throw of the dice. The following table shows the true odds against rolling any of these numbers. Since there are thirty-six possible combinations, the odds are figured by dividing the number of ways to roll any particular number into 36.

Chart 9
Odds of One Roll Bets

Number	Ways to Roll	Odds Against On Single Roll
2 or 12	1	35-1
3 or 11	2	17-1
7	6	5-1

Any Seven

Any Seven pays off at 4 to 1, whereas the true odds are 5-1 against a seven being rolled on the next roll, giving the house a 16.67% edge. Sometimes the bet is paid off at 5 for 1, which is the same as 4-1. When you see a "for" between odds numbers, reduce the first number by one. Therefore, 5 for 1 means 4-1.

Any Craps

The true odds against rolling either a 2, 3 or 12 on a single roll is 8-1, but the casino only pays 7-1, giving it an 11.1% edge.

The 2 or 12

If you bet that the next roll of the dice will be a 2, the odds are 35-1 against this happening. The same odds apply to a 12, since there is only one way to make either number. The casino pays only 30-1 on these wagers, giving it an advantage of 13.89%.

The 3 or 11

The true odds against rolling a 3 on the next throw of the dice is 17-1. The same odds apply to the 11, since either can only be made in two ways. The house pays off at only 15-1, giving it an advantage of 11.1%.

Horn Bet

This bet is often seen in Atlantic City or Northern Nevada, and requires 4 chips placed on the 2, 3, 11 and 12, and since the casino pays off at its usual bad odds if any one is rolled, you're getting four bad bets at once. Don't make a horn bet.

Other Proposition Bets

The Hardways

These aren't one-roll bets. When a player bets on a **hardway** number, he is wagering that the number will come up hard rather than easy, or before a 7 is rolled.

A hardway is the number 4 coming up as 2-2, the 6 coming up as 3-3, the eight coming up as 4-4 and the 10 coming up as 5-5. In other words, with these four numbers, they'll come up hard if identical spots show on each die.

If a 4 is rolled as a 1-3, it's an **easy** number. Remember, the easy ways and the 7 defeat a hardway bet.

Hard 4 and Hard 10

The true odds on these bets are 8-1, but the casino pays off at 7-1, giving it an 11.1% edge. Don't make the bet.

Hard 6 and Hard 8

The true odds on these bets are 10-1, but the casino will only pay 9-1, giving it an edge of 9.09%. This bet should never be made.

18.   Winning Craps Play

There are two ways to approach a craps table. One is to bet with the dice, hoping they'll pass, that numbers will repeat, and that the come-out roll will feature a lot of 7s and 11s. A bettor who wants the dice to pass is known as a **right** bettor. There is no moral interpretation of the term. It simply designates a player betting with the dice.

A player who doesn't want the dice to pass, who bets don't pass, is looking for a lot of craps, 2s and 3s on the come-out and a lot of 7s after a point is established. This bettor is wagering against the dice and is known as a **wrong** bettor.

The odds are roughly the same whether you bet right or wrong. You have an equal chance of winning, but remember, casino craps is a negative game, and only luck and correct and smart play will make you a winner. If you make foolish bets, that is, bets in which the house has a big edge over you, there's hardly any chance to walk away a winner from a casino craps table.

Right Bettors—Correct Play

A right player should only make bets which give the house its minimum edge. Therefore, the best and most conservative method of play is to make a pass-line wager, and if a point is established, to take the maximum odds allowed on that point. If uncertain about how much you can wager as an odds bet, ask the dealer.

Then, if the player wants to have a little more action, he can make a come bet or two come bets, also taking the maximum free-odds.

Betting this way, a lucky or hot roll of the dice can win a bit of money, and the player is only giving the house 0.8% in a single odds game and 0.6% in a double odds game.

This kind of gambler will be known as a *tough* player, because he's making only the best bets, and giving the house very little in the way of an edge. If lady luck shines down upon him, he can make a good bit of change with this method.

For the more aggresive bettor, after making a pass-line and one or two come bets, all with maximum free-odds, he can then cover the 6 or 8 if they're not already bet, by making place wagers on these numbers. Here the player will be giving the casino a bigger edge, 1.52%. But if the dice pass and some long rolls develop, the gambler betting this way can make a lot of money.

But don't under any circumstances make any other bet, no matter how tempting the payoffs may be. The house edge is just too great, and will wear

down your bankroll in no time flat. Craps is a fast
game, and a game in which you can lose your money
fast. So be careful and bet smart, in the manner we
suggested.

Wrong Bettors—Correct Play

The wrong bettor should make a don't pass bet
and then lay *single* odds against the point. Even
though double odds will slightly reduce the house
edge from 0.8% to 0.6%, a series of repeated points
and the player's bankroll will quickly disappear.

Then the wrong bettor should make one, and if
he's more aggressive, two don't come wagers, lay
single odds against the come points, and stop.

Those are the only bets a wrong bettor should
make.

To Summarize

Right Bettors:
Most Conservative:
1. Pass-line wager and full odds.
2. One come bet with full odds.

Conservative:
1. Pass-line wager and full odds.
2. Two come bets with full odds.

Aggressive:
1. Pass-line wager and full odds.
2. Two come bets and full odds.
3. Place bet on uncovered 6 or 8, or both.

If a come bet is repeated and won during the course of a roll, then make another come bet immediately. In other words, the most conservative bettor will have a come bet always working, that is, being bet or in action. The conservative bettor will have two come bets always working, as will the most aggressive player.

Wrong Bettors:

Most Conservative:
1. Don't pass bet, laying single odds.

Conservative:
1. Don't pass bet, laying single odds.
2. One don't come bet, laying single odds.

Aggressive:
1. Don't pass bet, laying single odds.
2. One don't come bet, laying single odds.
3. A second don't come bet, laying single odds.

19.   Money Management

Money management is an integral part of any successful gambling method. First of all, you should never play with money you can't afford to lose, or that would cause you financial or emotional discomfort if you lost it.

Gambling should be a fun thing, and exciting, but it can't be that if you're too emotionally involved. If that's the case, do something else, but don't gamble.

But, if you can handle the action, then divide your bankroll by fifty and that should be your unit for betting purposes. In other words, if you bring $50 to the table, don't bet more than $1 as your basic unit. With $100, this means $2 bets. Only if you have at least $250 should you be betting $5 at a time.

This is conservative, but will allow you to stay at a craps table for a long time, and may allow you to catch a hot roll, if you're a right player, or a long cold table, if you're betting wrong.

Try to double your money, and if you do that, quit. That's a good win in craps. If you can't do that, and you find you're winning $50 when you brought $100 to the table, and it's choppy, going nowhere, leave.

Another good time to leave is at the end of a hot roll, if you're a right bettor. Hot rolls don't come often.

Or, conversely, if you're betting wrong, and the dice are ice cold, with only craps and point numbers coming out on the come-out, and then 7s killing the point numbers time after time, leave when the dice start to turn, when 7s and 11s begin to show on the come-out and a point is repeated.

What if you're losing? Set a limit to your losses. The best way is to play with a bankroll you can afford to lose in that session of play. If you lose your one-session bankroll, leave the table. Above all, don't reach in for money after you've lost what you had in the rails.

The first loss is the cheapest. There'll be other games, other times. There'll always be time for more action at craps. Don't make the mistake of taking one terrible loss at one table. That's not the way smart gamblers handle losses.

Leave a winner if possible. A small win is better than any loss. You can't go wrong leaving a winner, remember that. Let's win!

20.   Glossary of Craps Terms

Any Craps—A one-roll wager that the next throw of the dice will come up 2, 3 or 12, craps numbers.

Any Seven—A one-roll wager that the next throw of the dice will come up a 7.

Back Line—Another term for the **Don't Pass** line.

Bar the 12 (or 2)—Making either number a standoff for wrong bettors, thus enabling the casino to keep its edge on don't pass and don't come bets.

Betting Right—Betting that the dice will win, by wagering on the pass-line and come.

Betting Wrong—Wagering that the dice won't win, or won't pass by betting on don't pass and don't come.

Big 6 and Big 8—An even-money wager that the 6 or 8, whichever is bet, will come up before a 7 is rolled.

Boxman—The casino employee who is in charge of an individual craps game. He is seated between the two dealers on base.

Buy the 4 and 10—Paying a 5% commission so the payoffs on these place numbers will be at 2-1.

Change Color—Changing casino chips into smaller or larger denominations.

Chips—Also known as **Casino Checks**—The tokens, usually of clay composition, that are used instead of cash by the players.

Come Bet—A wager made after the come-out roll, with the same rules as govern a pass-line bet.

Come-Out Roll—The roll that establishes a point for don't pass and pass-line bettors.

Craps—The term for the numbers 2, 3 and 12; which also gives the game its name.

Crap Out—The rolling of a 2, 3 or 12 on the come-out.

Crew—The dealers who staff the craps table.

Dealer—A uniformed employee of the casino who is either on base or a stickman at the craps table.

Dice—The cubes marked from 1 to 6 which, when rolled by a shooter, determine all wins and losses in the game of casino craps.

Die—The singular of dice.

Disk—Also known as **Buck, Marker Puck**—A white and black round object which shows whether there's a come-out roll coming up, or, if placed, shows the point number.

Don't Come Bet—A wager against the dice made after the come-out roll, subject to the same rules as a Don't Pass bet.

Don't Pass Bet—A wager prior to the come-out roll that the dice won't win, or pass.

Double Odds Bet—A free odds wager which is double the underlying bet.

Easy Way—The rolling of either 4, 6, 8 or 10 other than as a pair.

Edge—The advantage the house has on any wager. Also known as **Casino Advantage** or **Vigorish**.

Even-Money—A payoff at odds of 1-1.

Field Bet—A one-roll wager that the next number thrown will be a 2, 3, 4, 9, 10, 11 or 12.

Floorman—A casino executive who supervises one or more craps tables.

Free-Odds Bet—A wager made in addition to an underlying bet that is paid off at correct odds.

Front Line—Another term for **Pass-Line**.

Hardway Bet—A wager that the 4, 6, 8 or 10 will be rolled as a pair before they're rolled easy or a 7 is thrown.

Horn Bet—A one-roll wager combining the numbers 2, 3, 11 and 12.

Hot Roll—A long series of dice throws where the pass-line and right bettors win.

Lay Wager—Betting against a point number showing by paying a 5% commission.

Layout—The imprinted surface of a craps table, showing all the wagers that can be made, divided into separate areas.

Off—A term to signify that certain bets will not be at risk on the next roll of the dice.

On Base—The term for the dealers other than the stickman.

One-Roll Bets—Wagers determined by the next roll of the dice.

Pass—A winning decision for the right bettors.

Pass-Line Bet—A wager that the dice will win, or pass, made before the come-out roll.

Place Bets and Numbers—The wager that either one or more of the following numbers will come up before a 7 is rolled. The Place Numbers are 4, 5, 6, 8, 9 and 10.

Pit Boss—The casino executive in charge of all the craps tables comprising a craps pit.

Point, Point Numbers—The numbers 4, 5, 6, 8, 9 or 10 established on the come-out roll.

Press, Press A Bet—Increasing a winning bet, usually by doubling it.

Proposition Bet, Center Bet—Those wagers which are made in the center of the layout.

Rails—The grooved area on top of the table where players keep their chips.

Right Bettor—A bettor who wagers that the dice will pass, or win.

Seven-Out—The rolling of a 7 after a point has been established, losing the pass-line wager.

Shooter—The player who is rolling the dice.

Single-Odds Bet—A free odds wager equal to the underlying bet.

Stickman—The dealer who controls the dice and also calls the game.

Tip—A gratuity given to a dealer by a player. Also called a **Toke.**

Working—A term that the bets are at risk on the next roll of the dice.

Wrong Bettor—A player who wagers that the dice will lose by making Don't Pass and Don't Come bets.

Four.
Video Poker

21. Introduction

Video poker machines have been on the gambling scene a comparatively short while, but in that span of time their popularity has grown enormously. Many people think they're the same as slot machines, but there's a big difference. With slots, there's no decision making process, while at video poker you have to make correct plays to win.

Having skill at this game pays off, especially when there are jackpots involved. The payoffs can be lucrative, running into the thousands of dollars. And the game can be beaten even without hitting the big payoffs for it's structured so that, assuming best play by the gambler, it is practically an even-up game with the casino!

In this book, we're going to introduce you to the fascinating world of computerized video poker, showing the various machines you can play, how to play them correctly, and how to be a winner at this game!

22. How to Play Video Poker

Introduction to Poker Hands

For those of you who don't understand poker but want to play video poker, we'll briefly show the varying kinds of hands in descending order of strength, with the best hand listed first.

Chart 1: Poker Hands

Royal Flush - A K Q J 10 of the same suit.

Straight Flush - Any five card sequence in the same suit, such as J 10 9 8 7. Also A 2 3 4 5.

Four of a Kind - All four cards of the same value such as 7 7 7 7.

Full House - Three of a kind combined with a pair, such as 4 4 4 Q Q.

Flush - Any five cards of the same suit, but not in sequence.

Straight - Five cards in sequence, but not in the same suit, such as Q J 10 9 8. Also A 2 3 4 5.

Three of a Kind - Three cards of the same rank, such as 10 10 10.

Two Pair - Two separate pairs such as 8 8 3 3.

One High Pair- Any pair Jacks or better.

One Low Pair - Any pair below Jacks.

No Pair - Five odd cards

Some machines contain wild cards, such as a deuce (2) or a Joker. With these machines, Five-of-a-kind hands are paid off, such as a 9 9 9 9 Joker. This hand ranks below a Royal Flush.

Video Poker is basically draw poker, with all cards dealt out by the machine's computer. Five cards are dealt to the player and are shown on the screen. The player then has the option of holding or discarding as many cards as he wants thus he can hold all five cards or discard all five cards. Or he can hold on to four cards. After he discards some or all of his cards, these are replaced by other cards. He now has drawn to his hand and this final hand determines whether or not he or she is a winner.

For example, let's suppose that a player has received the following cards at the outset of play:

♠ Q ♦ 7 ♣ Q ♠ 3 ♥ 6

He has been dealt a pair of queens, which he will hold, while discarding the rest of the cards. That is his best chance of getting the strongest possible hand after the draw. He now discards the 7, 3 and 6 and receives three new cards. Let's assume that his hand now looks like this after the draw:

♠ Q ♥ Q ♣ Q ♠ K ♦ 4

He has improved his hand to Three-of-a-Kind, which means a bigger payout. The stronger the poker hand, the better the payoff.

The machine deals out cards from a 52 card deck, and will never deal a card previously discarded on the same hand. Thus, if a player gets rid of the 6 of clubs, he can't get it back after the draw.

The final hand determines whether or not the player

has won or lost. The board will flash **Winner** and show the kind of winning hand it was, such as Three-of-a-Kind, and the payoff. If the hand ended up as a losing hand, nothing will be flashed on the board.

An important consideration, one that should always be kept in mind by the player, is that, although this is draw poker, it is not being played against other players. It is played against the machine, and all one has to do is get hands sufficient for a payoff.

A mistake many experienced draw poker players make is thinking they're beating other players. They'll retain an Ace and get rid of a King, for example, whereas holding both is better to get a payoff in some situations. Or they'll discard a small pair, such as 3s, when those cards should have been held in some situations.

In regular draw poker, it might not pay to hold a low pair, but often, as we shall see later, it's the best play in Video Poker. Always keep in mind that you want to be paid off by the machine, not other players, and therefore, you'll have to alter your strategy to this effect.

Step by Step Play

When you sit down at a Video Poker machine, you'll encounter a number of buttons which allow you to do various things at the machine. But first of all, to make the machine operative, you have to put some coins in.

Video Poker machines take from one to five coins at a time.

We suggest that you always play five coins, never

less. On all machines, in order to hit the best payoff
on Royal Flushes, it is necessary to have played five
coins. If you only have three coins left, go and get
more coins, for if you hit the Royal Flush, you'll end
up with a much smaller payoff than you should have
received. Remember this and remember it well - five
coins at all times should be played.

After you put in the five coins, the screen will
automatically show five cards dealt in sequence, one
next to the other. If you hadn't inserted five coins, but
only one to four coins, for example, then in order to
have the cards dealt, you'll have to press a button
called **Deal/Draw**. Then the five cards will show on
the screen. But, if you put in five coins, the cards will
automatically be dealt.

Once you see the five cards, you'll also note that
the screen will show the various payoffs for various
hands to one side of the screen.

The payoffs increase in proportion to the coins
played. For example, if Two Pair pays 2 coins for
each coin inserted (2 for 1), after five coins are put in,
the payoff will read: "Two Pair - 10."

This means that if your final hand is Two Pair,
you'll get back or receive credit for 10 coins.

Now let's get back to the five cards shown on the
screen. Under each card, on the outside of the machine itself, will be a button that says **Hold/Cancel**.
Thus, there will be five of these buttons.

Let's assume that your dealt cards are as follows:

◆3 ♥6 ♣7 ♠10 ♥10

The best possibilities here are the two 10s, which
can be improved in various ways. To hold the two

10s and get rid of the other cards, you press the Hold/ Cancel button under each 10.

What if, by accident, you also pressed the Hold/ Cancel button under the 3? In that case you press it again, and the Cancel feature will kick in. It will not be held. How can you make sure of what you've held and not held? The word "Held" will show under the cards you've held. Here's how it would look with the previous hand:

♦ 3   ♥ 6   ♣ 7   ♠ 10   ♥ 10
                      HELD   HELD

Now that you're satisfied with your held cards, you press another button, called the Deal/Draw button. This will allow you to draw cards to the two 10s. The 3, 6 and 7 will disappear from the screen and will be replaced by the newly drawn cards. Your final hand may look like this:

♣ J   ♣ A   ♦ J   ♠ 10   ♥ 10
                      HELD   HELD

You've drawn Two Pair, and the screen will show **"WINNER - Two Pair 10"**, showing that you've ended up with a win of ten coins.

Credits

Most machines will allow you to take credits for the coins won, rather than getting the coins back after each win.

Here's how it works.

After the above win, there'll be a place on the machine for Credits. You'll see **Credit - 10**.

At the same time, a button on the outside of the machine will light up. It's called a **Cashout** or **Pay-**

out button.

Unless you desire to cash out by pressing this button, the coin credits will stay in the machine, and you can play them out, rather than collect them and put them back into the coin slot. This makes for much faster play, no fumbling for coins, and no dirty hands.

As you continue winning, the credits will increase, and the screen will always show you just how many credits you have.

To continue playing, without inserting additional coins, you now press another button, which may have different names such as **Maximum Bet** or **Bet 5**, but it will be plain that this lit button allows you, by simply pressing it, to use up 5 of your credits.

When you press it, three things will happen.

First, your screen credit total will now read Credit 10 (reduced by 5 from 15). Secondly, the possible winners on your next round of play will flash on one side of the screen, and thirdly, five cards will be dealt to you as the next hand.

You then play the five cards as you did before, trying to get the best possible hand for a payoff from the machine.

What happens if you've been dealt a complete dud, five cards that are low in value and mismatched (called **rags**), so that you don't want to hold any? You simply press the Deal/Draw button and all five cards will disappear from the screen to be replaced by five new ones.

What if the five cards you've been dealt at the outset are such that you don't want to draw any cards to the hand? For example, let's assume that you've been dealt the following hand:

◆4   ◆A   ◆3   ◆9   ◆8

You have five diamonds showing, a Flush, an immediate winner, without having to draw additional cards. What you do now is press the Hold/Cancel button under each and every card shown, till there are five HELDS on the screen.

Then you press the Deal/Draw button, and you will see WINNER - Flush as well as the number of coins you've won, flash on the screen.

If you have an immediate winner, such as a Flush, before the draw, *you must hold all the cards to get a payoff.* If you don't press all the Held buttons, and simply press Deal/Draw, the winning cards will disappear from the screen and you'll get five fresh cards.

Now, for the ultimate. What if you end up with a Royal Flush? You'll see **WINNER - ROYAL FLUSH 4000** on the screen. Lights will flash, and the full jackpot of $1,000 (4000 quarters) will be paid to you in cash.

If no one comes by, ring for a change girl or stop one when she goes by. She'll call for a casino executive to verify your win. Then you'll be paid in cash.

If it's a progressive machine the screen will show WINNER - ROYAL FLUSH PROGRESSIVE PAYOUT or a similar statement depending on the machine. If the payoff is above a certain figure ($1,200 on a 25 cents machine) you'll be asked to furnish a social security number and positive identification, and you'll be handed the cash along with a W2-G form to be filed with your next year's income tax.

But let's say that you didn't hit the jackpot but

have been winning steadily and now you're tired and want to get away from the machine. The credit reads 125.

You press the CashOut or Payout button and the coins will be released from the machine and drop into the well at the button of the machine. You take them over to a Cashier and they'll be counted and you'll get cash for them.

Go over the steps again carefully.

When you get to a Video Poker machine familiarize yourself with the buttons on the machine. If there's another button you don't understand the function of, ask a change girl to explain it to you. If she doesn't know, she'll get someone from the casino to help you.

Now that you're familiar with the Video Poker machine, let's move on to the most common of the machines, the one that originally made this game so popular, the Jacks or Better Video Poker Machine.

23. Jacks or Better

Jacks or Better in Video Poker refers to a pair of Jacks, Queens, Kings or Aces. Since the Queen, King or Ace is of a higher rank than the Jack, any pair consisting of these cards is known as Jacks or Better, or a High Pair.

If you get a pair of Jacks, Queens, Kings or Aces as your final hand, five coins will be paid back to you. For example, suppose you end up with a pair of Queens. You'll be declared a WINNER and be given credit for five coins.

Although you're not making any profit since you invested five coins, these returned coins really add up and contributes to making this game almost even-up with the casino when played properly. And we'll show you how to do this.

Once you master Jacks or Better, you'll be able to play the other games of Video Poker more intelligently, and we'll discuss those games in future sections. But the Jacks or Better machines is the one you're most likely to encounter, since they're the most popular of the Video Poker games.

There are two types of Jacks or Better machines, known as the **Full-Payout** or **Flat-Top** machine, and the **Progressive** machine. The Full-Payout will pay you a fixed amount of coins if you hit the Royal Flush - four thousand coins, provided that you played all five coins.

With the Progressive machine, you'll be paid a jackpot consisting of the amount shown on the Progression, which begins with 4,000 coins or $1,000 on the quarter machines and goes up from there. So, in most cases, if you hit the Royal Flush on the Progressive 25 cents machine, you can expect to cash in from $1,000 to about $3,000, and sometimes more.

There are also slight differences in the payouts between the two machines. Let's first examine the Full-Payout or Flat-Top Machine

Jacks or Better: Full-Payout Machine	
(Full-Payouts per coin)	
Royal Flush	800*
Straight Flush	50
Four of a Kind	25
Full House	9
Flush	6
Straight	4
Three of a Kind	3
Two Pair	2
High Pair	1
*(To receive the full payout for a RoyaFlush, 5 coins must be played)	

Note that five coins must be played, and should always be played, to receive the 800-1 payout for the Royal Flush. All of the payouts mentioned above are to 1 coin. Multiply this by 5 to get the real payout when you play that many coins.

For example, the Royal Flush will pay out 4,000 coins or $1,000, for a quarter machine. Getting a Straight Flush will pay you 250 coins or $62.50 and getting a Full House will pay you 45 coins or $11.25 for that same quarter machine.

These machines are known as 9-6 machines, because of the 9 payout for the Full House and the 6 coin payout for the Flush.

By High Pair, we mean Jacks or Better. A pair of 10s will not pay anything back, nor will any lower pair.

Jacks or Better: Progressive Payouts	
(payout per one coin)	
Royal Flush	Progressive Jackpot*
Jackpot Straight Flush	50
Four of a Kind	25
Full House	8
Flush	5
Straight	4
Three of a Kind	3
Two Pair	2
High Pair	1

*(Five coins must be played to get the full payout for the Royal Flush)

This machine is known as an 8-5, because of the payouts for a Full House and a Flush. Again, all payouts shown are for one coin, and so multiply the payout by 5 when five coins have been played.

Always play 5 coins with Progressive machines. Always.

The progressive machines start with a jackpot of $1,000, on quarter machines, exactly the maximum payout on the Full-Payout machines, and goes up from there. The machines are tied to a bank of machines feeding the progressive Jackpot every time a Royal Flush isn't made. Usually about 1% of the money fed into the machines is added to the jackpot each time the game is played. It slowly but surely builds up.

The total of the Jackpot is shown above the bank of machines on a flashing screen. It increases until someone gets the Royal Flush after putting in five coins. If a Royal Flush had been made while someone held less than five coins, the full jackpot is not won and the progression keeps building.

Progressive machines are available, as are Full-Payout machines in 5 cents, 25 cents and $1 denominations. On a 5 cents machine the jackpot starts at $200, and on the $1 machine it begins at $4,000.

To compensate for the progressive aspect of the machine, the payout on the Full House and Flush have been reduced to 8 and 5 instead of the 9 and 6 on the Full-Payout machines.

Winning Strategy
for Jacks or Better Machines

These machines can give you an even-up chance with the house, whether playing the Full-Payout or Progressive machines. But you must play them correctly.

So, let's go step-by-step, showing various hands that will be dealt, and how to draw to these hands. Study this section carefully, for it is the key to winning at Video Poker.

A. Going For The Royal Flush

Our first goal is to get the Royal Flush, so each time there's a possibility of this occurring, we have to weigh the hands dealt against the chances of drawing to the Royal Flush.

1. Whenever we have four cards to a Royal Flush, such as ♣K ♣Q ♣J ♣10 we discard the fifth card, even though it has given us a flush or a straight. For instance, we would discard any other club or any other ace in the above example, except the Ace of clubs.

2. In the above example, if there was another King, Queen, Jack or Ten, giving us a High Pair, we'd discard it, going for the Royal Flush.

3. When we have three to a Royal Flush, we should discard a High Pair and instead draw to the remaining three to a Royal. This is in line with our goal of trying to get that Royal Flush whenever possible. We want to get that big win.

For example, we're dealt ♦A ♥A ♥K ♥10 ♣3.

We'd go for the three cards to a Royal Flush in this situation, breaking up the high pair by throwing away the ace of diamonds (and club three), and keeping the ten, king and ace of hearts.

However, if we hold the following pat hands (hands that already have a payout on all five cards dealt) we don't go for The Royal Flush.

a. Straight Flush
b. Four of a Kind
c. Full House
d. Three of a Kind

4. When holding a small pair (10s or below) and three to a Royal Flush, we paired the card and go for the Royal Flush. Example: ♠Q ♠J ♠10 ♦10 ♥4. We discard the diamond 10 and heart 4.

5. When we have two to a Royal Flush, we hold all pairs over the possibility of going for the Royal Flush. For example, if we hold ♥A ♦A ♦Q and two rags (cards that can't help us) we retain the Aces rather than retaining the two diamonds.

If we hold a low pair and two to the Royal, we still hold onto the low pair, and discard the two cards to the Royal.

6. With two to a Royal, we hold onto four flushes and four straights, Three of a Kinds and Two Pair rather than going for the Royal Flush.

7. If we have two to a Royal and another high card, but no pair, we discard the other high card.

For example, suppose we're dealt ♣Q ♦A ♣K and two rags (small unmatched cards). We discard the diamond Ace and the rags, going for the Royal with our Queen and King of clubs.

So, always keep that Royal Flush in mind. It gives us the really big payout, and it's always there lurking in the machine. We can't afford to pass up the opportunity to go for it when the situation favors us.

Straight Flushes, Flushes and Straights

Our best payoff, other than the Royal Flush, is the Straight Flush. However, its payout is merely 50 for 1, or 250 coins against the Royal Flush's payout of 800 coins for 1, or 4, 000 coins. Therefore, although we're likely to get a Straight Flush four times as often as a Royal Flush, the payout is only 1/16 of the Royal Flush, and even less than 1/16 if a Progressive Jackpot hits.

For example, if the progressive jackpot is $2,000, twice the minimum of 4,000 coins, then the payout on the Straight Flush would be 1/32 of the Royal Flush.

Although we must be aware of the Straight Flush, it's not something we're constantly looking for, as in the case of the Royal.

When we are dealt a Flush, and it contains four to a Straight Flush, such as ♥10 ♥9 ♥8 ♥7 ♥2, our best play is to retain the Flush and not go for the Straight Flush.

If we are dealt a Straight, and it contains four-cards to a Straight Flush within it, we stand pat with the Straight. An example would be ♠7 ♠6 ♠5 ♠4 ♦3

A High Pair is always preferable to a four to a Flush or four to a Straight. We retain the High Pair (Jacks or better) and break up the possible Straight or

Flush.

With a low pair, we break up the low pair (10s or lower) in favor of the four to a Flush, but we retain the low pair and break up the four to a Straight.

Four of a kinds, Full Houses and Three of a Kinds

Four of a Kind hands pay half of what Straight Flushes pay, but occur much more frequently, about once in every 420 hands, or about 22.7 time more frequently than the Straight Flush. Since it pays half of what the Straight Flush pays, it's a much better value for us, coming up so frequently.

Generally, Four of a Kind hands come out of the blue and surprise us. We start our hand with a High Pair or a low pair, and boom! out come two more of the same rank, giving us Four of a Kind. Or we may stay with Three of a Kind and we get the fourth of that rank. Sometimes, we'll really be surprised by staying with but one high card and getting three more for a Four of a Kind hand!

This is the main difference between regular Draw Poker and Video Poker. In the regular game, we wouldn't stay in with low pairs or just one high card, because it will be a loser in the long run. In Video Poker we have nothing to lose, for we've already invested our money.

Three of a Kind hands occur about once every thirteen times we're dealt hands, or about 7.5% of the time. We may get them by retaining a low or High

Pair, or start with Three of a Kind. Or perhaps, if we're fortunate, we've stayed in with one High Card and received two more of the same rank after the draw.

We always stay for the draw with a Three of a Kind hand. It's much stronger for us than three to a Royal Flush, so if we're dealt ♥K ♥Q ♥10 ♣10 ♦10, we retain the three 10s and discard the King and Queen of hearts.

A Full House is often made from a hand that starts as a Three of a Kind hand. Or it may develop from a Two Pair hand, where the odds are roughly 11-1 against this happening.

Of course, like all hands in Video Poker, a Full House may come out of the blue, where we've retained one low pair, such as ♦5 ♠5 and see the draw produce ♣J ♦J ♠J

A Full House occurs a little over 1% of the time.

Two Pair, High Pairs and Low Pairs

Two Pairs occur about once every 7.6 hands and pays off with only two coins for one invested or in reality, even-money. Thus, we get back 10 coins for the five coins we played, the five we invested plus the five won.

We always retain an original hand of Two Pair hoping for a Full House at best, though the odds are about 11-1 against this occurring.

A High Pair allows us to get our original investment back each time the hand comes up. Although this doesn't seem like much, it is the reason for the game's popularity, for it enables players to constantly get payouts and thus retain their bankroll till the big payouts come through. Never underestimate the power of the High Pair. We should be dealt one about every 4.6 hands.

We retain the High Pair when it is part of a possible Straight or Flush, and discard the other cards in those situations.

However, if there's four to the Royal Flush or three to the Royal Flush, the High Pair would be discarded in favor of possibly getting the Royal Flush.

If the High Pair is part of a Straight Flush, such as ♦J ♦10 ♦9 ♦8 ♣J then we get rid of the club Jack in this situation and go for the Straight Flush. We also do this even if the possible Straight Flush can be made by drawing to it as an inside Straight Flush, as in the following situation:

♥Q ♥J ♥10 ♥8 ♠Q

In the above example, the spade Queen would be thrown away. There's a chance for a Straight Flush, a Flush, a Straight, and another High Pair when this is done, giving us more powerful hands to go for, with bigger payouts.

With small pairs, we have hands that give us a great many payouts when they are improved. Normally, in regular draw poker, only a very weak player would retain a pair of deuces, but in Video Poker, those deuces can turn into Three-of-a-Kind hands or better if we get a lucky draw.

When do we retain small pairs? First of all, if the rest of the hand is blank, (filled with rags, trash cards of no value to us). For example:

♠3 ♦10 ♥8 ♥5 ♣3

The best we have here is the pair of black 3s. We'd hold the 3s and draw to them.

If the low pair comes as part of a Flush, we discard the odd paired card and draw to our four Flush, as in the following example:

♣7 ♣9 ♣3 ♣A ♦9

We get rid of the diamond 9 and draw to the remaining clubs hoping for a Flush.

However, if we have a Low Pair and it's part of a possible Straight, we hold onto the Low Pair and draw to it, such as ♦6 ♠6 ♦7 ♣8 ♣9

In this case, we discard the 7, 8 and 9.

We also discard the Low Pair if the remaining cards are three to a Royal Flush.

If we have a Low Pair, and it's part of a three to a Straight Flush, as in the following example, we retain the Low Pair.

♣8 ♣7 ♣6 ♦6 ♥2

The correct play is to hold the pair of 6s.

Other Hands

Most of the time, the hands dealt to you at the outset of play, before the draw, won't be winners by themselves. You'll have to improve thcm to get a payout. Some of the hands will be so bad that you'll discard all five cards and draw five new ones.

At times you'll find yourself with a beautiful drawing hand that comes up empty. For example:

♠A ♠Q ♠J ♠K ♦3

Having four to a Royal Flush, we discard the diamond 3 and draw, hoping for the BIG ONE! Instead, we draw a 9 of hearts and end up without a payout of any kind.

Other good hands will end up as blanks for us. This is to be expected. Don't get discouraged. There will be other times, as there was for this author, when the following hand was dealt to him at the outset:

♦4 ♥7 ♦9 ♠2 ♣J

Faced with this pile of garbage, I retained the Jack of clubs, the only viable play. Imagine my surprise when I drew and the screen showed the following:

♣K ♣Q ♣10 ♣A ♣J
                HELD

And on the screen was the flash of WINNER! JACKPOT! ROYAL FLUSH!

That can happen, so the big ones that get away shouldn't stop you from continuing to play. Sooner or later, your lucky moment may come.

When dealt hands that aren't immediate winners before the draw, we first have to look for the possibility of a Royal Flush. For example, if we're dealt the following:

♣3 ♦10 ♠6 ♥9 ♦K

We save both the King and 10 of diamonds. We have two to a Royal, and that's our best shot, even though, if the 10 gets paired, we won't get our money back. We're always looking for the Royal.

Many times we'll get a hand like this:

♦4 ♥A ♣J ♠6 ♥3

We hold the Ace of hearts and Jack of Clubs here, for we're trying to pair one of these to get our coins back. Many Players make the mistake of retaining only the Ace and discarding the Jack. That's a bad play. Hold onto both.

The reason they make this common error is that they think they're back playing Draw Poker against friends - where retaining the Ace because it's stronger than the Jack might be playable.

But in Video Poker, the Ace has no more value than the Jack; either paired will get our coins back.

Here are a listing of other hands that should be drawn to when dealt at the outset. None of these are immediate winners.

1. Four to a Flush.

2. Four to a Straight.

3. Four to Straight Flush, whether the missing card is on the inside of the possible Straight Flush or not. For example, ♥9 ♥8 ♥7 ♥5 and a rag. Go for the Straight Flush here. Of course since you have a Four to a Flush, you'll automatically draw to this hand in the proper way.

4. Three to a Straight Flush. If you're dealt cards that contain at least three to the Straight Flush, discard the rags and go for it. If the hand contains a high card as part of the Straight Flush, it is that much stronger, such as ♣J ♣10 ♣9, since the Jack may be paired.

5. A low pair. We've touched on this hand before. It's a very common starting hand, and can develop into a monster after the draw. Just because it doesn't pay automatically doesn't mean you get rid of it. When dealt the following:

♣5   ♦5   ♥A   ♣J   ♦10

We retain the pair of 5s, which are stronger for us than the Ace of hearts and Jack of clubs.

Now let's deal with those hands that are so bad there's no reason to hold any of the cards. When we get five blanks or rags, we discard all the cards and go for five new cards on the draw. A typical hand might be this:

♥2 ♦6 ♣10 ♦5 ♥9

There's nothing worth holding. We don't save two to a Straight or two to a Flush, or even, in this situation, two to a Straight Flush. They're just not strong enough hands. We don't save the highest valued card of the five, the club 10, because even if it's paired, it won't give us any return. We discard all the cards, and draw five new ones.

To do this, simply press the Deal/Draw button and five new cards will appear on the screen.

If the 10 of clubs had been the Jack of clubs, we'd have retained the Jack. If paired, it would return our money.

Don't be afraid to get rid of all five cards if they're weak and start with five new cards after the draw. There's always the possibility of getting a payoff of some kind, or even a tremendous payout after a draw like that. I saw someone get Four of a Kind drawing to five new cards. It's even possible to get a Royal Flush when doing this!

Some Winning Hints

We have discussed the fact that Video Poker is a different game than regular Draw Poker. One of the important differences is this - when you play Draw Poker at home or in a casino and you're dealt five cards, the first thing most players do is sort their cards.

If they've been dealt a pair, they put them together. If they have four to a Straight, those cards are placed together in sequence.

However, when playing Video Poker, the cards come up on the screen just as the computer deals them, and the player can't sort them out by hand, only in his or her mind. So, you've got to be super-careful about not overlooking a strong hand. Here's an example of a hand I saw a player overlook before the draw:

♦ 5   ♥ 6   ♣ 3   ♦ 2   ♠ 4

Dealt these five low cards, he pressed the Deal/Draw button immediately to draw five new cards, overlooking a straight.

Or the hand might look like this:

♣ 4   ♦ 3   ♠ A   ♥ 5   ♣ 2

In this situation a player told me he saw someone hold the Ace and get rid of all his other cards, overlooking a Straight.

Therefore, my best advice is to slow down a bit and examine the cards that have been dealt at the outset and see just what you have on the screen. Take your time in determining the correct play.

Remember, if you make a mistake, and hold a card you don't want to hold, you can rectify that mistake by pressing the Hold/Cancel button, and the card will no longer be held. As long as you don't press the Deal/Draw button, you still have a chance to change your mind.

Even experienced veterans of the game make mistakes. They may be weary or tired or upset and they can, in this state, overlook obvious plays. If you reach a point where the game has become tedious, leave the machine and cash in. Take a break and a rest and go back another time

Practicing At Home

To familiarize yourself with correct play in Jacks or Better, my advice is not to go to a casino unless you've practiced the game at home. To do this is simplicity itself. Get a standard deck of cards and remove the Jokers. This leaves you with 52 cards. Shuffle them thoroughly and then deal out five card hands to yourself, one at a time.

After you've dealt out five cards, look over the hand and decide what to hold and what to discard. For example, you might deal this hand:

♣A   ♦3   ♦6   ♥K   ♣9

In this situation, you'd hold the club Ace and the heart King and discard the other three cards.

Discard the cards by putting them aside, not back in the deck. When you play Video Poker, the machine will not deal you a card you've already discarded, and neither should you do this at home.

Then draw three cards. You may take them right off the top of the deck or shuffle up the remaining cards and pick out three at random. It really doesn't matter how you do this.

After you've dealt out the three additional cards as your draw, see what has developed, whether or not you'd have gotten a payout. You can keep a record of your wins and losses, meanwhile refining and correcting your play.

After you're comfortable with the game and feel

you know what you're doing, then you can go to a casino and play for real money.

Testing Your Knowledge of Jacks or Better

The following is a small quiz to refine and test your knowledge of the game played in the casino. We'll assume we're at a Progressive Jacks or Better machine with an 8-5 payout on the Full House and Flush, respectively.

Decide how to play each of the following hands:

1. ♣5 ♦5 ♠A ♠9 ♦10

We hold the pair of 5s and discard all other cards. Players are tempted to hold the Ace as a "kicker" hoping to pair it, but don't hold kickers in Video Poker. It's a losing proposition.

2. ♦9 ♦K ♣K ♠8 ♦2

We hold the two Kings and get rid of all the other diamonds. Our best play when facing a four to a Flush with a High Pair, is to retain the High Pair.

3. ♣K ♣A ♣Q ♣10 ♠J

With four to the Royal Flush, we discard the spade Jack. Whenever we have four to a Royal we're going for that big payout. Break up the Straight in this situation.

4. ♠Q ♦3 ♠J ♥K ♥2

This is a common situation. We have three High cards, but two of those are of the same suit. In this situation, we get rid of the High card not of the same suit. Thus, we'd hold the Queen and Jack of spades and dump the heart King. We're giving ourselves a shot at the Royal Flush and giving up the chance of pairing the King in this situation. Of course, we're giving up a three to a Straight, but going after the Royal is a better bet.

5. ♠9 ♠5 ♠2 ♣8 ♣3

We hold nothing out of this pile of garbage. Even though we have three to a Flush, there's no reason to overcome the great odds in getting the flush by drawing two to it. We're better off going for five fresh cards after the draw.

6. ♠10 ♣8 ♦3 ♠J ♠4

At first glance, it would seem that we hold the spade Jack and discard the other cards. Or we should take a long shot and hold all three spades. Both of these decision are incorrect. What we have to do here is hold both the spade Jack and the spade 10. although the 10, if paired, gives us nothing, the 10 and Jack gives us two to the Royal. A much stronger play than merely holding the spade Jack.

7. ♠2 ♠A ♣K ♦J ♣2

We hold the deuces and discard the three big cards. A small pair is powerful in Video Poker. There's a possibility of getting Two Pair, Three of a Kind, a Full House and even Four of a Kind. When we have a small pair, we don't chase after the possibility of pairing a big card. And we don't hold kickers.

8. ♥Q ♥J ♠10 ♠4 ♠3

With this hand, we have three to a Flush and three to a Straight. However, we also have a Queen and Jack, which, if paired, will get our coins back. We therefore hold the Queen and Jack and discard the other cards.

9. ♠K ♣9 ♠J ♠Q ♥9

Here we have three to a Royal Flush plus a small pair of 9s. Whenever we have this situation a low pair opposed to a three to a Royal, we get rid of the low pair and hold the three to a Royal Flush.

10. ♥K ♥Q ♥10 ♥J ♥5

Here we have four to a Royal Flush, as well as a formed Flush. In this situation, we get rid of the heart 5 and go for the Royal Flush.

Why? Just look at the odds. Suppose the Progressive payout at this point is $1,600 for $1.25 or 1,280 for 1.

Even though we already have the Flush in hand, the chances of getting the Ace of hearts and completing our Royal is only 46-1. We know five of the 52 cards, and thus, with 47 cards remaining, one of them is the Ace of spades. We're taking a chance at winning 1,280 for 1 by going for a 46-1 shot.

We could go on and on with the quiz. However, you can test yourself by playing out hands at home as advised in the Practice At Home section. If you practice enough, there are sure to be all kinds of hands that you'll have to pause and think about. Study our book and you'll know what to do, so that, by the time you get to the casino, you'll be ready to play correctly.

24. 10s or Better

This type of machine is rarely found in casinos. Sometimes only $1 machines can be found. There are occasional Progressive machines available with very low payoffs on the regular hands other than the Royal Flush and they're generally avoided by experts.

The following is the payout on the non-progressive machines. Note that the Royal Flush is paid at 800-1 only if five coins have been played.

10s or Better - Full Payout	
Royal Flush	800
Straight Flush	50
Four of a Kind	25
Full House	6
Flush	5
Straight	4
Three of a Kind	3
Two Pair	2
High Pair (10s to Aces)	1

This machine pays off only 6 units for a Full House, compared to 9 units on the Jacks or Better machines, and only 5 units instead of 6 for the Flush. However, this is made up by returning the coins played whenever the players gets a pair of 10s.

Play is pretty much the same as for Jacks or Better; however, 10s are retained instead of discarded as they are in Jacks or Better.

25. Deuces Wild

Like the other versions of Video Poker, the game is played with the 52-card deck used without the jokers. However, each of the four deuces (2s) is a wild card, which means that it can be used as any card in the deck, not only in rank (such as a 5 or 6, for example) but as any suit.

Thus, a 2 of clubs can be transferred, if needed, to an Ace of spades to complete a Royal Flush. Since there are four deuces in the deck, hands containing at least one deuce have been calculated to occur about 35% of the time.

The following is the payout for Deuces Wild Video Poker. Note that the Royal Flush as a natural hand (without the deuces) will be paid off at 800-1 only if five coins are played.

Deuces Wild Video Poker Payout	
Royal Flush (Natural)	800
Four Deuces	200
Royal Flush (deuces)	25
Five of a Kind	15
Straight Flush	9
Four of a Kind	5
Full House	3
Flush	2
Straight	2
Three of a Kind	1

After the normal arrangement of hands in Jacks or Better Video Poker, the Deuces Wild version of Video Poker must seem upside down. For example, the weakest possible hand with a payout is Three of a Kind. And a Five of a Kind hand pays only 15 for 1! With the deuces running wild in the deck, all kinds of crazy hand can be made.

Playing Deuces Wild can be a roller coaster ride with wild streaks coming and going, both favorable and unfavorable. When the deuces show up on the screen, all kinds of payouts are possible. When they're absent, it's a desert out there, because of the low payouts on relatively strong hands, such as 2 for 1 (even-money) for a Flush.

With Deuces Wild, you must be patient and not get discouraged with a long losing streak. Even if dealt one deuce, your chances of making a hand that pays out is only 54%.

With three deuces, you can expect to have some

very strong hands, with about 80% of them being Four of a Kind or stronger.

Strategy for Deuces Wild Video Poker

First and foremost, when we have a deuce or deuces dealt to us, we must evaluate our hands carefully for the strongest possible hands. Very powerful hands in deuces wild aren't obvious with deuces showing, so pay careful attention to the following hands.

1. If we have three deuces and two to a Royal Flush, that's a Royal Flush and should be held intact.

2. With two deuces and three to a Royal Flush, that's a Royal Flush and should be held intact.

3. Two deuces and Three of a Kind is a Five of a Kind hand and should be held intact.

4. If we have two deuces and three cards to a Flush, it is a Flush (and possibly a Straight Flush) and should be held intact.

5. Two deuces and any pair gives us Four of a Kind and should be held intact.

a. With two deuces and three odd cards, none of which can give you a Royal Flush, draw 3 cards to the deuces.

b. With two deuces, if you have 2 other cards to a Royal or Straight Flush, and one blank, discard the blank and go for the Royal or Straight Flush.

c. With 2 deuces and any single card (10, J, Q, K or A) that will give you a Royal Flush, retain this card.

6. With a single deuce and three to a Royal Flush

plus a blank, we discard the odd card (blank) and draw. Example: 2 A♣ K♣ J♣ 4 ♦ we discard the 4 of diamonds and draw one card.

7. Without a deuce, if the hand is pat, that is, already assures us a payout with all five cards involved, we hold all five cards and do not draw.

8. Without a deuce, we hold four card Straights and four card Flushes and four card Straight Flushes and draw.

9. Without a deuce, we hold three card Straight Flushes, and draw.

10. If we have been dealt Two Pair at the outset, we discard one of the pairs. We do this because Two Pair doesn't pay anything. With One Pair retained, we can improve that to Three of a Kind or higher valued hands with our without the addition of a deuce.

Many of the hands in Jacks or Better became money payout hands just by pairing a high card (a Jack or better). In Deuces Wild, these hands have no value to us. Getting One Pair or even Two Pair gives us nothing but a loser. We must constantly strive for the big hands. If we have a deuce or more than one deuce we must study the situation carefully to get our biggest possible hands, then play for those big hands.

Now, what do we do with weaker hands? For example, suppose we're dealt the following hands:

♥A ♦K ♣Q ♦4 ♥9

We'd get rid of all five cards in this situation. Our goal is to get at least a Three of a Kind hand and none of these cards will help us. High cards have no preference over low cards here - there's no special coin return for High Pairs.

Suppose we have the following hand:

♥Q ♦K ♣9 ♠5 2

Again, we discard all the cards except the deuce. Having a high pair does us no good. Three cards to a Straight or Flush does us no good. We hold the deuce and hope for the best.

You're going to find yourself getting rid of all five cards in Deuces Wild quite often, as much as 25% of the time. This is to be expected, since we need that big Three of a Kind hand just to get our coins back.

Play the game correctly and you'll be rewarded with all kinds of big hands, and if you encounter a good winning streak, this game can earn you some good money even without hitting the Royal Flush.

26. Jokers Wild

In casinos you're going to come across this game played in two versions. The first is known as **Ace-King** and the second as **Two Pairs**. In the first version of the game, any pair of Aces or King will get our money back, while in the second version of the game, the minimum winning hand is Two Pairs.

With the addition of the Joker, we now have a deck containing 53 cards, with approximately 10% more different kinds of hands dealt out than in the standard 52 card Video Poker games.

Since there's only one joker, the hands aren't as complicated to figure out as Deuces Wild Video Poker, where all four deuces run rampant. Still, it's a more complex game, with a more complicated payout scale. Let's examine the payouts, and as usual, keep in mind that the Royal Flush can only be paid off with the maximum return if five coins are played.

Joker Wild Payout (Ace-King)	
Royal Flush (natural)	800
Five of a Kind	200
Royal Flush (Joker)	100
Straight Flush	50
Four of a Kind	20
Full House	7
Flush	5
Straight	3
Three of a Kind	2
Two Pair	1
Ace or Kings	1

Note that there's the same payout whether one gets a pair of Aces or Kings, or Two Pair. The most popular of the Joker Wild game in this version is played as a 25 cent machine.

A version of the above game which should be avoided by players, features only a payout of 15 for 1 for Four of a Kind. Don't play this machine, but look for one with a full payout of 20 for 1.

Joker Wild Payout (Two Pair)	
Royal Flush (natural)	1000
Five of a Kind	100
Royal Flush (Joker)	50
Straight Flush	50
Four of a Kind	20
Full House	8
Flush	7
Straight	5
Three of a Kind	2
Two Pair	1

The lack of payout for any hand below Two Pair makes this a machine many experts avoid. When the Joker doesn't appear at the outset, before the draw, there are going to be many hands that will not get any payout whatsoever.

The machine, however, is available to be played for 5 cents, which makes it popular despite the tough payout schedule. And some machines have a Double Up feature, which allows the player to take the original payout or try for a double or nothing situation. Since a double or nothing option gives the house no advantage, being a 50-50 proposition, the return is increased to the point where it is almost an even game with the casino.

Joker Wild - Aces and Kings Strategy

The Joker will appear in the hand less than 10% of the time, or about 9.4%. Without the Joker present there will be many instances where the five cards dealt at the outset will have to be discarded. Since only Aces and Kings are good as High Pairs, we don't retain Queens or Jacks. They're as useless as very small pairs.

When playing without the Joker present at the outset, we will break up a Straight to go for the Straight Flush. Thus, a hand consisting of ♥9 ♥8 ♥7 ♥6♣5 will be broken up. The 5 of clubs will be discarded and one card drawn to the hand.

If we have a three to a Royal Flush, we prefer that hand to a pair of Aces or Kings. For example, ♦J ♦A ♦Q ♣A ♠5 will be broken up as follows: The spade 5 and the club Ace will be discarded and we'll go with our three to a Royal Flush.

Without the Joker, not only will many hands be discarded, but the following hands should also be completely discarded, with nothing held for the draw:

a. Two cards to a Flush

b. Three cards to a Flush, unless it gives us a chance at a Royal Flush, such as A J 10, or a Straight Flush, such as 9 7 6.

The strategical considerations for this game are complicated by the fact that there are often two different ways to play the hand; one with the Joker and one without.

There is a strong likelihood of getting Straight Flushes with the Joker. Therefore, a Joker which forms a Flush will be broken up if there's a possibility of a Straight Flush. Such a hand would be:

Jkr ♥7 ♥6 ♥5 ♥Q

We get rid of the Queen and forfeit the 5 for 1 payout in the hope of getting the 50 for 1 payoff for the Straight Flush.

A similar situation occurs when we have Jkr ♦5 ♦6 ♦J ♣9. Here we discard both the Jack of diamonds and the club 9 going for the possible Straight Flush with the Joker and the two other remaining low diamonds.

Likewise, a Straight containing the Joker will be broken up in favor of a four card Straight Flush.

With a Joker present at the outset of play, we have many chances at a Straight Flush and should keep this in mind. For example, if we have a Joker with a high card (Ace or King) we break it up if there's a possibility of getting a Straight Flush even if we only have three to the Straight Flush. An example of this would be Jkr ♦A ♣9 ♣8 ♠7

In the above instance, we discard the diamond Ace and Spade 7 and draw for the Straight Flush. We would keep a Straight made with the Joker unless there is a possibility of getting a Straight Flush by having four to the Straight Flush. An example of this hand is the following:

♠7 Jkr ♠6 ♠5 ♦4

We discard the diamond 4 and try for our Straight Flush. Again, we give up the chance for a 5 for 1 payout in favor of the possible 50 for 1 payoff.

Many times, when dealt the Joker with other cards, we'll discard all the other cards and play for the draw with just the Joker remaining. This will happen about 10% of the time and will include the following hands:

a. The hand, including the Joker, only contains three cards to a Flush. Keep the Joker only.

b. The hand, including the Joker, only contains two card to a Straight Flush. Keep the Joker only.

c. There's no chance for a Royal Flush.

Most of the time we'll be playing hands that go for the Straight Flush or Royal Flush. Or we'll be going for Flushes and Straights, holding three cards with the Joker. We'd hold Three of a Kind hands, Straights and Full Houses, together with stronger hands, of course.

Jokers Wild is a good game to play, because it's essentially an even game with the casino. But you must master it by studying this section carefully, to get your best shot against the house.

Winning Strategy for Joker Wild - Two Pair

This is a very tough game to beat when the Joker doesn't show up. The need for Two Pair for a payout gives the casino its biggest edge over the player in any of the Video Poker games, unless the Double Up feature is present. That feature allows us to go for double or nothing after play, and brings the machine up to the standard of other Video Poker games, with less than a 1% edge to the house.

Like its partner, the Jokers Wild game, there is a strong likehood of getting Straight Flushes and the strategy for going for them is identical to that game.

One big difference. A Straight won't be broken up to go for a potential Straight Flush, unless there's also the possibility of getting a Royal Flush. With the Joker giving us three cards to the Royal Flush, we hold that in favor of a four to a Flush, four to a Straight and a single Pair.

When a Joker is dealt in this game, we should avoid playing it alone, as we do in the Ace and King version of Joker Wild. It is to our advantage to hold onto the Joker and a 10, Jack, Queen, King or Ace and go for the Royal Flush.

Three to a Straight Flush or Royal Flush are important hands for us to play to the draw, especially if we haven't yet been dealt the Joker. The Joker gives us a wide opportunity to fill in the Straight and Royal Flushes.

27. Money Management

You'll be encountering Video Poker machines that take nickels, quarters and dollars. By far, the most common and popular machines are the 25 cent ones. They offer a good payout, and the risk of losing big money is much less than the $1 machines.

The Bankroll

When playing any kind of machine, whether 5 cent, 25 cent or $1 ones, we suggest that you have sufficient funds to carry you through a long session of play. To do this, we advise our players to have at least 200 coins of whatever denomination they're playing. With nickels, that amounts to $10; quarters will require a $50 investment, and dollars a $200 bankroll. This will give you sufficient play for quite a while, unless you hit an immediate crushing losing streak, which is very rare.

However, you have the chance of hitting a winning

streak as well, where you'll start with credits after playing the first five coins and never have to dig in again. You can't know what the future brings in terms of gambling; you have to see what happens, and play the very best you can.

There's another good reason why you should have this many coins. You may be onto a good machine that you feel is going to feed you the Royal Flush. Perhaps you've come close a few times, with four to the Royal showing up.

You just feel in your bones that it will happen soon - that big payout! But you find that you started with only twenty or forty coins and now you have to find a change girl or go to the cashier's cage across the casino to get more coins.

If you have to get up, and there's someone sitting next to you, you may have to ask them to hold your seat. If they agree, to further strengthen your claim to the seat, you may invert a container that holds coins, and put it on the seat Then you get up and go for the additional coins.

However, when you come back, someone else is sitting in that seat, and the neighbor, a stranger you didn't know, shrugs his or her shoulders, or is no longer playing. And while you're standing there getting ready to argue, the guy in your seat hits the Royal Flush!!!

That's a nightmare come true. So, give yourself leeway with enough coins to carry you through a long session. Start with even more coins, 400 coins. All it is is some additional weight,which you can put away in the well of the machine or in a nearby container. If you don't use up the coins, just cash them in at the end of play. The casino doesn't care. They'll take them back without question.

Of course, before you play any machines, make sure that you can afford to lose the money you're gambling with. Although these machines will give you a chance to break even with the house, short term fluctuations may swing wildly one way or another.

When to Quit

A principle of gambling that is wisdom to all concerned is "the first loss is the cheapest." If you start with your bankroll of 100 coins and lose it, quit. Something is wrong with your luck that day, and you don't want to take a big single beating that you will find hard to make up.

If you're winning, then you have to decide just when to quit. There are several factors that may play a role. First of all, you may be at a machine that is seducing you with fours to a Royal Flush coming up time and time again. If you have a feeling that it may come up, keep playing even though you're winning big. By big, we mean upwards of 150 credits. With the credit feature of the machine, you can easily see just how you're doing.

If you feel fresh, keep playing the machine. But if you find yourself making mistakes through fatigue, stop playing, no matter how much you're winning or losing. It's time to take a break or pack it in for the day. Don't fight fatigue.

To insure a winning session, when you hit the 150 credits mark, you may want to put away 50 of those coins, and play the remainder of the 100 left. Since the payout button doesn't work that way, but pays out all the credits, you simply make a mind decision to stop when the credits hit 100, then cash out.

If you hit the 200 mark after making this decision, you can up the win to 125. If the machine turns cold and gets down to 125, you cash out. If the machine, however, continues hot, with all kinds of big hands coming up one after the other, stick with the machine.

Maybe it will get up to 350. By then, you've decided to cash out when the machine fall to 275. By making these mind stops on the way up, you'll have the advantage of playing on with the "hot" machine, and being assured of leaving the machine a winner.

But again, do this only if you don't get fatigued and make mistakes.

If you never reach that 150 mark, but hover around the 60-100 mark in winnings, you may decide that, if the machine drops to 50, you're going to cash out the credits. Again, you'll assure yourself of a nice win.

If the machine never gets above 50 in credits you may decide to leave when the machine credits drop to 0, so as to limit your losses to the few coins you've played.

The figures we've mentioned are just "ball park" figures. You may want to set a goal of 120 credits, for example, and then quit if it goes down to 60 or 70. Fine. You might want to cash it all in if you ever reach 200 credits. Not so fine. I'd always give myself some leeway. I'd set the mind goal at 30-40 credits below that figure if you're conservative and leave then (if the credits now are 160-170).

This is known as "stop-loss" playing, and those of you who own stocks know about this concept. You won't hit the top in winnings, but you'll give yourself the chance to keep adding to the winnings.

I've seen players move up like that, till they were in the 400 credit range, when their initial goal had been 150 credits. The machine was hot and kept hitting big hands. You don't get those kind of machines every day of the week, so take advantage of them.

What if you hit the Royal Flush? You'll be paid in cash by an executive of the casino for the Royal. After you're paid, look to see if there are still credits remaining in the machine. They're yours and shouldn't be left there in the excitement of the moment.

Cash in those credits (but only after you're paid for the Royal) and don't play that machine anymore. It's done it's job, giving you the Royal. Take a break and try another machine if you're still feeling lucky.

Play a machine in another area of the casino, and see if you can repeat your big win!

28. Selecting the Best Machine

Any type of machine you select, among those we've discussed, will give you about an even-money shot against the casino. Of course, you want more than that; you want to get a big win. Your best chance at this is to get the Royal Flush, and get it on a Progressive machine.

When you go into a casino, it'll look like a forest of metal, with slot machines predominating. If you don't see any Video Poker machines, ask a Change person to help you out. They'll know where they're located.

Then study the kinds of machines they have there. If they're some new exotic machine you don't understand, don't play it. But generally speaking, you're bound to find the Jacks or Better machines, which we feel is the easiest to play and gives as good a return as any other.

You may find one to two types of Jack or Better. There will either be the Full Payout type or the Progressive machine. Now, make certain that the coins denomination necessary to play the machine is within your bankroll.

If you're inexperienced, don't attempt the $1 machines. It might be better for you to practice on the 5 cent ones. Usually, the machine you'll encounter the most will be the 25 cent one.

If the machine is a Full Payout one, make certain that it is of the 9-6 variety; that is, it pays off at 9 for 1 on the Full House and 6 for 1 on the Flush. If it is a Full Payout machine and only pays off at 8-5 on those hands, don't play it. The house is taking too much of an edge.

If you find a Progressive machine, it will pay out at 8-5 for the Full House and Flush, and the jackpot for getting the Royal Flush will begin at $1,000.

The jackpot progressive amount will be displayed on a screen above a bank of machines tied up to that Progression. Since it begins at $1,000, if it shows an amount like $1,014.66 you can be sure the Royal Flush has been recently hit.

Try and play a progressive machine that's much higher than that in terms of the Royal Flush payout. A machine that shows $1,400 is better, of course, and even better is one that's $1,800 or over $2,000.

If there are only $1 machines available, and you either have a limited bankroll or don't want to risk that kind of bet, don't play the machines. If there are only 5 cent machines, and you want at least a quarter machine, don't play the 5 cent ones. You may have an attitude - "I just want to kill some time and lose a few bucks." That shouldn't be your stance - you should always think of making money at Video Poker.

Let's assume that you found a bank of Video Poker machines that is agreeable to you. They're Progressive Jacks or Better, played for 25 cent and the present Jackpot is over $2,000.

Get change for your cash, with sufficient coins to give yourself a long session with the chance of hitting the Royal Flush.

These progressives are extremely popular and you may find only a couple of seats open. Which of the two seats should you take? That's difficult to answer. You're there; you have to make the decision.

I watched a friend play at a Progressive machine in one of the downtown Las Vegas casinos. There were only two seats available and the jackpot was $1,666. The two empty seats were next to each other.

He hesitated and then selected one of them. He started to feed the machine coins and quickly used up a $10 roll of quarters. Nothing came up for him. Nothing.

Meanwhile, a middle-aged man took the other empty seat. He hit a Full House the first shot, then a Flush, then Three of a Kind, and two more Full Houses.

My friend meanwhile had used up $30 worth of quarters. He opened another roll, while looking around for a different seat.

"I hate this machine," he told me. "Look at this guy next to me. Why didn't I pick that machine. "

The man next to him had over 240 credits showing and continued to hit good hands.

My friend, with a disgusted gesture, put in his five coins, and out came the following hand:

   ♦Q ♣K ♣J ♥3 ♠4

He correctly discarded the heart 3, spade 4 and the diamond Queen, foregoing the possibility of pairing the Queen, against the possibility of drawing three to a Royal. Out came the following:

   ♣A   ♣K   ♣J   ♣10   ♣Q
     HELD HELD

Bells started ringing, and my friend was $1,666 richer.

So you never know. Some players jump around from machine to machine as their luck turns sour; others stick with the same machine. People are superstitious and many are afraid to switch machines, fearing that the person taking their place will immediately hit the Royal.

But you have to use your own instincts. And perhaps they'll be correct and you'll be grinning from ear to ear as the big payout comes along!

Five. Poker

29. Introduction

Welcome to one of the greatest games ever invented by man - poker!

Poker is one of the most fascinating of the gambling games, because it combines three elements: skill, luck and psychology. It is this combination which draws millions of players to the card tables around America to try their luck at poker.

Not only will you learn the most popular poker games, but with each game we also supply a great deal of strategy, which should give you an immediate edge over less skillful players. You'll learn which hands to go in with, how to bet, when to play aggressively and when to be cautious.

These strategies should make you a winner. And the games presented are those in which a great deal of money can be made by skillful players. You'll be learning the games by reading this book, but more importantly, you'll be learning how to be a winner.

30. The Fundamentals of Poker

Certain things are common to all poker games, and we'll now discuss them, so that, when we cover the individual games, you'll be familiar with these aspects of the game.

The Deck of Cards

All the poker games we're going to discuss in this book will be played with a 52-card deck, containing four suits of 13 cards apiece. The suits are both black and red. The black suits are spades and clubs; the red ones hearts and diamonds. In poker, the suits have no intrinsic value in determining winning hands. A flush in spades is not stronger than one in hearts, and a straight in clubs isn't weaker than one in diamonds.

The Four Suits

What is important is the rank of the cards. As we mentioned, there are thirteen cards in each suit. The highest ranking card is the ace, followed in rank by the king, queen and jack. These last three are called **face cards**, since, unlike all the other cards, they have pictures of people rather than spots and numerals to determine their value.

In the course of this book, we'll refer to the ace as A, the king as K, the queen as Q and the jack as J. All other cards, from 10-2, will be shown by the numeral; so that an eight will simply be shown as an 8. The numbered cards rank in value as follows, in descending order: 10, 9, 8, 7, 6, 5, 4, 3, and finally the 2, known as the **deuce**, which is the lowest ranking card of all.

Rank of the Hands - High Poker

Poker can be played as either high or low poker. Most of the games are played as high, such as **Seven-Card Stud, Hold 'Em,** and so forth. However, there is a game called **Lowball**, which is usually played as a draw game, or closed game, in which the cards are reversed in value, with the best card being the ace and the weakest card the king. This will be discussed under the rank of the hands - low poker. For now, we'll concentrate on high poker and show the relative ranks of the hands, in descending order, from best to worst.

Royal Flush

This is the top hand in high poker, and a player may see it only once or twice in his or her lifetime. The hand consists of the A, K, Q, J and 10 **all of one suit.** For example, if these cards were all diamonds, spades, clubs or hearts, it would be a royal flush. If the same hand were of different suits, it would have a weaker ranking, and simply be an Ace high straight.

Royal Flush

Straight Flush

This hand consists of five cards of consecutive rank, all of one suit, but with the top ranking card lower than an ace. For example, the K Q J 10 9 of diamonds would be a straight flush. Likewise the 5 4 3 2 A of clubs. For purposes of straights, as in a straight flush, the ace is either the highest or lowest card. Thus, a hand of 2 A K Q J and a hand of 4 3 2 A K would not be straight flushes.

Straight Flush

When two players have a straight flush, the one with the highest ranking card leading the hand would win the pot. A hand of 8 7 6 5 4 of clubs would beat out a hand of 7 6 5 4 3 of spades because the 8 is higher ranked than the 7. If both straight flushes are identical, the pot is split.

Four of a Kind

This hand contains four cards of the same rank, such as J J J J, along with an odd card.

Four of a Kind

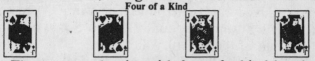

There cannot be ties with four-of-a-kind hands, and when two players have these hands, the highest ranked card wins the pot. Four 9s will beat out four 8s.

Full House

This hand consists of three-of-a-kind, combined with a pair. 999 AA; 666 KK and QQQ 22 are all full houses.

Full House

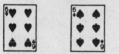

If two or more players have full houses, then the player holding the highest ranked three of a kind wins the pot. JJJ 99 will beat out 777 AA.

Flush

A holding of five cards of the same suit is called a flush. K Q 6 4 3 of diamonds would be a flush, and to identify it, it would be called a **king high** flush since its highest ranked card is a king. The best flush is an **ace high** flush.

Flush

When two players have flushes, the highest ranked card in the flush determines the winner. If both have, for example, a *queen high* flush, then the next ranked card determines the winner, and so forth, till a winner is found. 10 9 8 5 4 as a flush beats out of flush of 10 9 8 5 3.

However, if all five cards are identical, the pot is split.

Straight

Five cards in consecutive sequence but not of the same suit constitute a straight. For example, Q J 10 9 8 of mixed suits is a straight. An ace high straight of A K Q J 10 is the highest possible. The lowest possible straight is 5 4 3 2 A, with the ace here as lowest card.

Straight

The highest ranking straight wins when two players have straights. If both straights are identical, the pot is split.

Three of a Kind

This hand contains a holding of three cards of identical rank plus two odd cards. 333 K4 and QQQ 92 are three-of-a-kind hands.

Three of a Kind

When two players hold three-of-a-kind hands, the highest ranking wins. Three queens will beat out three jacks.

Two-Pair

This hand contains two separate pairs of identically ranked cards plus an odd card. AA 55 2 and QQ 88 K are two-pair hands.

Two Pair

If two players hold this kind of hand, then the highest ranking of pairs would win. If one player holds **aces up**, and the other **queens up**, as in the example of two-pair hands above, the aces up hand would win.

Should players hold the identical high pair, then the other pair is taken into consideration to determine a winner. Should both pairs be identical such as two players holding 77 22, then the odd card is examined and the highest ranking odd card wins. 77 22 5 beats out 77 22 4. If all five cards are identical, the pot is split.

One Pair

A pair and three odd cards make up this hand. 55 AQJ and 77 843 are both one-pair hands. If two players hold a pair, then the highest ranking pair wins. If it's identical, then the highest ranking odd card determines who wins the pot. 99 QJ8 will beat out 99 QJ7.

One Pair

If all five cards are identical, the pot is split.

No Pair

When a player holds five odd cards, not of the same suit, it's the weakest of all poker hands. When two or more players hold this hand, the highest ranked card wins the pot. If this is identical, then the next card is examined and so forth. J 9 8 5 3 beats out J 9 8 5 2.

If all five cards are identical, the pot is split.

Jack High Hand

To recapitulate: If there are several players at the showdown, which is the point where hands are shown to determine who wins the pot, then the highest ranking hand wins automatically. If one player has a straight and the other two have three-of-a-kind, the straight would win.

Object of the Game

To state it as simply as possible, the object of poker is to win the money in the pot. The **pot** is the accumulation of antes and bets made by the players. There are two basic ways to win the pot. The first and most common way is to have the best hand at the showdown. The **showdown** is the moment after all bets have been made on the final round of play. In high poker, the highest ranked hand wins the pot.

The other way is to force all the other players out of the game prior to the showdown, so that you are left alone in the game. At that point you can claim the pot and collect the winnings.

Forcing players out can be done by heavy betting, whether or not you have the hand to back up your betting. If you don't, that is known as **bluffing**, making it appear that you have a powerful hand by making big bets.

Study the rankings of the hands till you understand which hands are best, both in low and high poker. It's always amazing to see players who, after years of experience, still can't tell whether a flush or straight is a higher-ranked hand.

The Deal

In all poker games, there must be someone to deal out the cards to the participants. In private games, one of the active players does this. Each player in a private game gets to deal; and the deal moves around the table in clockwise fashion.

In the casino games, the house employs a dealer who deals the cards all the time. The players never deal in a casino setting. In those games in which the dealer has an advantage by acting on his hand and betting last, such as **draw poker** and **hold 'em**, a button is moved around the table clockwise, so that each player in turn is the imaginary dealer when he has the **button**, and receives the advantages of playing and betting last.

The dealer has several obligations. He or she must shuffle up the cards so that they are as random as possible when dealt out. The cards are usually given to the player to the dealer's right to be **cut**, that is, the top part removed and put to one side, after which the dealer restacks them with the bottom part of the deck now on top. In casino games, the dealer does this himself.

Then the dealer must make sure that all antes are in the pot before dealing. He must make sure each player gets the required number of cards or card on each betting round, and that all bets are correct.

The dealer also calls the game; telling which player is to bet first on any particular round, and at the showdown, the dealer examines the players' hands to determine who has won the pot.

Antes

An **ante** may be called a **sweetener**. Each player, when an ante is required, places some money or chips in the center of the table prior to the first betting round. Usually it is a small percentage of the average bet, and is placed in the pot in order to force more *action*, since there will be more money to be won even on the first betting round.

In casino games there is usually an ante for every

type of poker game. In private games, there is usually an ante only in the closed versions of poker such as draw poker.

Betting and Limits

Poker, after all, is a game played for money. Without money involved, it would be a dull game. All games have some kind of betting limit, which is usually two-tiered, such as $1-$2, or $5-$10 and so forth. Usually the higher limit is double the smaller one, but sometimes there is more of a spread, such as $1-$4.

A $1-$2 game means that all bets before the draw, including raises, are $1 and increments of $1; after the draw, $2 and increments of $2 when raising.

There is betting on every round of play, and the higher limit prevails at certain times, as will be shown in the individual games.

In casino games, the limits will be shown for each table, usually by a sign above the individual poker table. If in doubt, ask the dealer. In private games, the betting limits are set by the players prior to play.

In private games, chips or money may be used. Chips are always preferable; they're easier to handle and to stack, and they come in different colors, to denote different denominations. Cash is always green; and is cumbersome to place down and to stack.

In casino games, chips alone are used, except for coins. Usually the casino will use the same chips in general use for the other games. These chips usually come in $1, $5, $25 and $100 denominations. For antes and such, coins are used, usually 25¢ and 50¢ pieces.

When you go to a table in a casino, you will be required to get some chips. This is known as a **buy-in**, changing cash for chips. Usually there is a minimum amount you must buy-in for. The best rule is to have at least 40 times the minimum bet as your stake at the table. You don't have to have it all in cash. If you're at a $1-$4 table, for example, the buy-in required may only be $20. You can purchase $20 worth of chips and place $20 below that in cash on the table. That is your table stake. In casinos, you are playing **table stakes.** You can't take out more money from your pocket if you're involved in a game, and have to make a bet. However, you can always take out more money between deals and replenish your stake.

If you don't have enough *table stake* money to cover a larger bet, than you only participate in that part of the pot in which your money is already involved. The dealer will segregate subsequent bets into a different pot.

Betting Rounds

In the stud games, such as Seven-Card Stud and Hold 'Em, there are a number of betting rounds. In draw poker, whether Jacks or Better, or Lowball, there are only two betting rounds, one before and one after the draw. All this will be explained in the individual games.

After all the betting is completed, if there are two or more players in the game, then there is a showdown. That's when the players show their hands to determine who is the winner. If one player shows the best hand, the others may concede the pot without showing theirs. But if another player feels he has a stronger hand, then he or she shows the hand to claim the pot.

At the showdown, the player whose last bet or raise was called is the first to show his or her cards. Then the others in turn can show theirs.

Player's Options

Unless a bet is mandatory, as in the opening round of play, a player usually has a few options available to him. He may make the bet or he may pass or check. Passing or checking means not betting but having the option to see or call the other player's bet when it is his turn again.

Betting, like dealing, goes around the table in clockwise fashion. After a bet is made, the player whose turn it is can no longer pass or check and remain in the game. If he doesn't want to bet, he folds or discards his cards and is out of the game.

However, if he decides to stay in the game, he or she may call the previous bet, that is, make a bet of the same amount as the previous bet. Or he or she may raise the previous bet, by making a larger bet. For example, if the previous bet was $1, the player can raise by betting $2, the original call of $1, plus a $1 raise.

If the previous bet was a raise of another bet, then a player can reraise that raise. In casino games, there is usually a limit of three raises on any round of betting. If a player has previously checked his hand, he cannot raise when it is his turn to bet again, unless **check and raise** is allowed, where a raise is allowed after an initial *check*, which it usually is in casino play, but not in private games.

The Rake

In private games, no money is taken from the pot to run the game, but in the casino game, there is a **rake**, that is, money taken from each pot by the dealer, which is taken from the players and given to the house to run the game.

The rake varies from casino to casino. The smaller the game, the higher the percentage of the rake. Never play in a game with more than a 5% rake for the house. You'll be spinning your wheels in that game. Sometimes not only is there a limit on the percentage, but also the amount taken from each pot. For example, in some casinos where there's a 5% rake, no matter how big the pot is, no more than $2 or $2.50 may be taken out.

There's usually a sign near the table designating the rake. If in doubt, ask the dealer or the men who run the game in the casino. But you should know the rake before you sit down to play, and remember, make 5% the limit for yourself.

31. Seven-Card Stud

In **stud poker**, some of the cards are concealed, while others are seen by all the other players. In **seven-card stud**, there are three concealed cards, two dealt face down prior to the first betting round, and the final card dealt is face down, before the last betting round.

Seven-card stud is by far the most popular form of stud poker, and is one of the most popular poker games played privately and in the Nevada casinos. As we discuss the game, we'll show the differences in the private and casino game, which, though minor, lead to somewhat different strategies at times.

The Fundamentals of Poker section should be consulted as to the rank of cards and hands, object of the game and player's options, as well as the deal.

Play of the Game

In both the private and casino versions of the game, each player at the outset of play receives three cards from the dealer, dealt one at a time, with the first two cards dealt face down and the third card dealt as an open card. Then the first round of betting commences.

In the private game, because this game provokes a lot of action, there is no ante. In the casino game, there is an ante, usually 10% of the minimum bet. If it's a $5-$10 game, the ante is generally 50¢. In a smaller game, such as a $1-$4 game, the ante can be either 10¢ or 25¢, but this ante structure varies from casino to casino.

The ante is put into the pot by all players prior to the deal. Thereafter it becomes part of the pot and goes to the winner of the pot.

After each player has his or her three cards, the first round of betting begins. There are altogether five rounds of betting in seven-card stud. The first round is usually called **Third Street** because three cards are already in each player's hand.

Seven Card Stud—Third Street

On Third Street in private games, the high card opens the betting. If two players have an equally high card, then the player closest to the dealer's left with the high card opens the betting. For purposes of betting, let's assume that all the games are $5-$10. The opening bet in a private game will be $5, and the high card holder must make this bet. It is mandatory.

Thereafter each player in turn, starting with the

player to the opener's left must either see or call the bet or can raise the bet by making it $10.

If a player doesn't want to bet on this opening round of play, he is out of the game, and his cards are folded and handed to the dealer, who puts them to one side, out of play.

Let's see this in illustrative form. We'll assume there are eight players at the table in a private game. Player A is the opener. ** stands for the hole cards.

Player A.	**K	Player E.	**Q
Player B.	**3	Player F.	**5
Player C.	**10	Player G.	**9
Player D.	**4	Player H	**8

Player A puts $5 into the pot. Player B folds, by turning over his 3 and giving the dealer his three cards. Player C calls with a $5 bet. Players D, E, F and G also fold. Player H raises the bet to $10.

Now only Players A, C and H are in the game. It's now up to Player A. He can call the raise by betting an additional $5 into the pot, or going out. Or he may reraise. Let's suppose he reraises, moving the bet up to $15 by putting in an additional $10 (he already had bet $5). Now Player D has to bet an additional $10 to stay in the game. He makes the $10 bet and Player H adds another $5 to his bet to call Player A's reraise, and they're all in for the next round of betting.

The dealer now gives each player another open card. Player A is closest to the dealer's left and gets the first card. On this round the hands look like this.

Player A. **K Q
Player D. **4 4
Player H. **8 J

The highest hand now belongs to Player D. In stud poker, when there are two levels of betting as here, $5-$10, a player can open with a $10 bet only when there is an open pair showing, or on *Fifth Street*, even if there isn't an open pair. This round of play is *Fourth Street*.

On the second round of betting and on all subsequent rounds, the player with the high hand can either check his hand or make a bet. If he checks, he must call a bet or raise to stay in the game, but he can't raise after checking in a private game.

Here Player D checks, and Player H bets $10. Player A raises the bet to $20, and Player D calls the bet, but Player H now folds his cards, leaving only Players A and D in the game. There will be three more betting rounds, with the last betting round coming after they've each received a face-down card. Let's suppose it's now *Seventh Street*, the final betting round, and this is the situation.

Player A. **K Q 5 9 *
Player D. **4 4 3 A *

Player D is still high with his 4s. He bets $10 and Player A calls the bet. Now we have the showdown, since all the betting rounds are over. Both players will show their cards and the best hand wins the pot.

Player D, who was called, must show his cards first. He has 4 K 4 4 3 A J. Selecting five of those cards to form his best hand, it is 444 AK, three-of-a-kind.

Player A shows his hand, Q J K Q 5 9 10. His best hand is K Q J 10 9, a straight. Since a straight beats a three-of-a-kind, Player A wins the pot. If he had a weaker hand than Player D, he'd have the option of not showing his hand, by just conceding the pot to Player D.

We see now, in seven-card stud, that we use the seven cards dealt to us to form our best hand of five cards.

What we've just discussed is the private game. Now for the casino game. In this game, there is a fixed dealer, who always deals the cards, and he or she is a house employee.

In all games played in a casino, expect to have a rake. Usually the rake is about 5%. Sometimes it's more, very rarely less. In a number of games, although there might be a rake of 5%, there's also a limit of $1, $2, or $2.50 that will be taken out of the pot no matter how big the pot is.

In casino games, expect also to ante. We'll discuss the basic $5-$10 seven-card stud game here. The ante is 50¢, and the rake is 5% or $2.50, whichever is less.

All players ante before the deal. With eight players in the game, the ante comes to $4, money that is often fought for immediately with raises on the opening round.

In the casino game, the **low card opens.** This makes for more action, and the more bets there are, the more money the casino makes. Also, the game becomes a livelier and better game. A $5-$10 bet is usually much more conservative in a casino than in a private game.

Instead of low card betting $5, in the casino game, he can bet $1, but he must make this bet. Then he can be raised to $4, and thereafter the raises will be in $5 increments on the opening round, Third Street. On the other rounds, the betting will be $5 unless it's Fifth Street or an open pair shows, when the betting will be at a $10 level with increments of $10.

On the opening round, if two players have the same ranked low card, since the dealer is in a stationary spot, the player with the lower ranked suit opens. For purposes of opening on this round, and this round only, the suits, in descending order, are ranked, spades, hearts, diamonds and clubs.

Let's illustrate a game. ** = hole cards.

Player A.	**9	Player E.	**A
Player B.	**Q	Player F.	**J
Player C.	**3	Player G.	**4
Player D.	**5	Player H.	**K

Player C must open with a $1 bet. His 3 is low card on board. Player D, next in turn, folds. Player E raises to $4. Player F and G fold. Player H calls the $4 bet. Player A folds and Player B raises to $9 with an increment of $5 over the previous raise.

Now it's up to Player C, who folds. Player E calls by putting in $5 more. Player H also calls.

We now have Players B, E and H in the game. They each get another card on Fourth Street, and this is how their hands look.

Player B.   **Q A
Player E.   **A 9
Player H.   **K 2

Player B is high with A Q. He bets $5 and players E and H call. On Fifth Street the hands look like this.

Player B.   **Q A 6
Player E.   **A 9 4
Player H.   **K 2 K

Player H is now high with his kings, and he bets $10. Player B calls and Player E folds.

On Sixth Street the hands look like this.

Player B.   **Q A 6 3
Player H.   **K 2 K Q

Player H is still high and bets $10. Player B folds, leaving Player H alone in the game. He wins the pot, but doesn't have to show his hole cards. The game is over and the players ante before a new game is dealt.

Strategy at Seven-Card Stud

The first and most important strategy is what to stay in with on Third Street. Only stay in with three-of-a-kind, a three flush, a three straight, a high pair (10s or higher), or a lower pair with an ace, king or queen as odd card.

Don't stay in with any other hands. You might also stay in with a small pair, lower than a 10, if both are concealed, no matter what the odd card. But that's it.

On Fourth Street, if your three flush or three straight doesn't improve, get out of the game. Fold your cards. If a bigger pair shows than your pair, unless your odd card is higher than the pair showing, go out also. Don't stay in with second-rate cards. Only the best hand wins, not second or third best.

How to bet your cards? With three-of-a-kind, play them slow. Don't raise till Fifth Street. With a high pair (10s or higher) come out raising, unless you see that someone else has a higher pair. In that case, fold them. With a small pair and a high **kicker**, or odd card, call and try to improve on Fourth Street. If you don't improve and face higher pairs, go out.

With a possible flush or straight, even if you improve to a four flush or four straight on Fourth Street, you're still an underdog against a pair of kings. These are known as drawing cards (the four straights and flushes) and you call till you have made your hand, then raise.

That's the basic strategy. You want to have a possible winning hand by the showdown. If you're beaten on board, don't chase the other player. Only when your hand is strong and can get stronger enough to win, do you stay in. With good cards, play aggressively, with drawing cards, conservatively within the boundaries of the strategies mentioned above.

One final note: In the private games, once a player has checked, he can't raise. In the casino games, "check and raise" is permitted. It is useful on rare occasions, and shouldn't be used until you're an expert in the game, but be aware that it is the casino rule.

32. Texas Hold 'Em

Hold 'Em, as the game is also called, is one of the most popular and fastest growing games being played today, and can be found in many casinos, especially in Las Vegas. The game is usually played with 11 participants, and is a high action money game.

Play of the Game

In casino games, there's only one dealer, and there's usually an ante, though it can be rather small (less than 10%) of the minimum bet. Since the dealer is stationary throughout play, a button is moved around the table after each deal, and the person who had the *button* is the imaginary dealer, with the player to his or her left having to make the first bet.

A button is used because position is important in this game, and it is to a player's benefit to bet in a late position, seeing what the other players have done first before commiting himself.

In this game, there's usually a **blind. A blind bettor** must make a bet on the opening round of play, regardless of the value of his cards. This is done to promote action, and make the game more lively.

Usually the blind bet is less than the customary wager. For example, in a $5-$10 game, the blind bettor must open for $1 or $2, and he can then be raised to $4 (sometimes $5). Thereafter the betting is at the lower range of the game, $5, until a later round of betting. But rules of betting vary from game to game and casino to casino. Check with the dealer when in doubt about the betting or any other rules you aren't sure about.

The dealer deals out two cards to each player, both cards face down, and dealt one at a time. The first player to receive a card is the one to the left of the button; the last player to get his card is the button.

After each player has received his or her two cards, there is a betting round. Here the blind bettor opens, and then the betting goes around in turn, with each player having the opportunity to call the bet, raise it or go out by folding his cards. No player can check on this round.

After all bets have been made, the dealer will turn up three cards on board. These are community cards, used by all the players equally to form their best hands. Altogether there will be five cards on board, but the players will only receive their original two closed cards, no more.

Hold 'Em—The Flop

The three cards dealt face up on board are known as the **flop**. Altogether five cards will be on board, and the players will use three of these, combined with their own two cards, to form their best high poker hand, for Hold 'Em is a game of high poker.

After the flop, the betting continues for another round. Here, the first player to bet is the blind. If he's folded, the player still in the game who's closest to the left of the button. Then the betting goes around in clockwise fashion, with any player able to open the betting. If it's a $5-$10 game, the opening bet must be $5. After the bet has been opened, any player may call, or raise or fold. Raises are in $5 increments.

Then there's another card put out on board. Now we have another betting round, called Fourth Street, with the bets now moving into the higher range; $10 in a $5-$10 game. After this round, another card is dealt face up on board, and now we have the final betting round, known as Fifth Street.

After all bets are made on this round, and if there are two or more players remaining in the game, there's a showdown, with the best high hand winning the pot.

Strategy at Hold 'Em

There are two aspects to strategy at Hold 'Em. The first is the cards to stay in with, and the second is the position you're in at the table. Let's now examine the best cards to stay in with. There are really three groups; the very best, strong and marginal hands.

In Hold 'Em you're going to get only two cards at the outset, and then you're going to have to eventually share all the board's cards with the other players at the table. If you improve, they may also improve. So, from the outset, you want to have the kind of hands that can win at the showdown, when all the bets have been made and the players show their hands to determine the winner of the pot.

Very Best Hands

These are the best possible hands to hold prior to the flop, in descending order. When we speak of *suited* we mean both cards are of the same suit.

A A	
K K	Q Q
A K (suited)	A Q (suited)

With these cards you're going to be aggressively raising no matter what position you're in, right from the beginning. It may turn out that even these powerful hands will be weakened when the flop comes out, but unless the flop contains a four-flush or four-straight in which you have no involvement, or shows three-of-a-kind, where the fourth card may be held by one of the other players still in the game, you want to raise and force the other players to submit to your bets in the hope that they won't draw out on you, that is, draw cards that will beat your hand.

Strong Hands

We'll look at these in descending order.

A K (not suited)

A Q (not suited)   A 10 (suited)

A J (not suited)   K Q (suited)

Why are the ace hands so strong? Because a pair of aces is generally boss in Hold 'Em. Suppose you hold K Q of diamonds and the flop comes up 9 of spades, 6 of diamonds and a 4 of clubs. At this point you're not even the favorite. One of the players against you probably has an ace in his hand. Perhaps two players hold an ace. If Fourth Street comes up with any card but a diamond, king or queen, you're dead now. You have to pray for a king or queen on Fifth Street. If you don't get it, forget about these cards. Even a flop of K of spades, 10 of clubs, 5 of hearts followed by Fourth Street of 2 of diamonds and Fifth Street of A of clubs buries you. That ace is a *scare card*, and you can figure that at this moment someone has combined for at least aces with an ace in his or her hand.

Marginal Hands

These are listed in descending order.

J J

10 10   9 9

A J (not suited)   8 8

A 10 (not suited)   Q J (suited)

K J (suited)   J 10 (suited)

With these cards, you have to be careful, hoping to stay in cheaply for the flop, so that you can draw cards to improve your hand. Suppose you stay in with K J suited in clubs, and the flop comes up A of spades, 4 of diamonds and a 3 of hearts.

At this point, you have to expect another player to have at least a pair of aces. You are dead here and must throw away your cards.

This leads to another principle of Hold 'Em. Try and get your big bets in before the draw if you have the very best cards, to prevent the strong and marginal hands from hanging around to see the flop.

The next most important consideration is position. The earlier you have to bet or act on your hand, the weaker your position. The later, the stronger your position.

Take advantage of position by betting aggressively with strong hands or by staying in cheaply with marginal hands. The better your position, the easier it is to stay in for the flop.

For example, if you hold J J, a marginal hand at best, and you're in 10th position at the table, your position is great. If there have been a few raises to you, throw away the cards. If you are able to get in cheaply, by all means do so. If you're in early position, let's say 3rd, and you call the opener, if there are a few raises behind you, don't stay in. You're facing big hands, and if any scare card comes out, which for you is a Q K or A, you know you're a heavy underdog with your jacks.

Also gauge your opponents, and find out who stays in with weak hands and who plays tight. This, together with position and good cards, will make you a winner.

33. Draw Poker - Jacks or Better

This is a closed variation of high poker, also called **Jackpots**. By closed, we mean that all the player's cards are unseen by the other participants, whereas, in stud poker, some of the cards are seen by all players. In Hold 'Em, the player has two **pocket,** or closed cards, but all the community cards are exposed. However, in draw poker, they're all hidden.

Play of the Game

There is usually an ante, whether this game is played at home, in a casino or a club, since draw poker is legal in the California Clubs. The ante is usually about 10% of the maximum bet, which, in a $5-$10 game, would be $1. However, antes vary from game to game and casino to casino.

The best game is with eight players, and each player gets to deal in a private game. The dealer has an advantage, for he or she gets to bet and act last. Position is of great importance in draw poker.

In the casino games, where there is a stationary dealer, a button is moved around the table clockwise, so that each player, in turn, gets the button and is the imaginary dealer.

Each player is dealt five cards face down, one card at a time, after all the antes are in the pot. Then, the player to the left of the dealer or button is the first to act.

In draw poker, there will be two betting rounds; the first occuring before the draw and the second after it. The draw, as we shall see, allows players to discard cards from their hands and get new ones from the dealer in an attempt to improve their holdings.

In the game of jacks or better, a player can only open the betting if his hand contains at least a pair of jacks, or a higher-ranked pair or a higher-ranked holding. Thus, a pair of 10s can't open the betting, but queens can. And any stronger hand than a pair of jacks, such as three of a kind, a straight and so forth, can open the betting.

If a player's hand is weaker than jacks, he or she must check on this opening round. The players in turn may check until one player can open the betting. After the opener has bet, then each player in turn, starting with the player to the opener's left, can either fold and go out, call the bet, or raise the bet.

Let's follow a game to see how this is done.

Player A.	Q J 7 6 4	Player E.	A J J 4 2
Player B.	A 7 5 4 2	Player F.	3 3 3 9 6
Player C.	J 10 9 8 4	Player G.	Q 10 6 5 2
Player D.	K K 8 5 2	Dealer	7 7 A 6 3

Players A, B and C must check, since they don't have openers. Player D opens the betting with $5. Player E folds. Though he has jacks, he knows they have little value, since Player D had to have jacks or better. Player F raises to $10. Player G and the dealer fold. Player A and B fold, and Player C, who has a four-straight, calls the $10 bet. Player D puts in $5 more to call Player F's raise.

Now there are three players remaining in the game, C, D and F. At this point, there is a draw. Each player in turn, starting with Player C, the player closest to the dealer's left, may draw as many cards as he wishes to improve his hand. He draws one, throwing away the 4 face down, and is given one card by the dealer. Player D throws away three cards, retaining the kings, and is dealt three cards face down by the dealer. Player F draws two cards, retaining his three 3s, and gets two cards face down from the dealer. Now there is another betting round.

At this point, let's see how the hands look.
Player C. J 10 9 8 9
Player D. K K 8 8 10
Player F. 3 3 3 K 7
The opener is first to bet in the second round. Player D. checks. He may do this and still come into the betting later. Player F bets $10, the higher range of the $5-$10 game, which comes into effect after the draw. Player C, who didn't get his straight folds.

Player D, with two pair, and afraid Player F is bluffing, calls the $10 bet.

Now all betting rounds are finished. Player F, who is called, shows his three 3s. Player D concedes without showing his cards, for he is beaten. He may do this. If he had stronger cards than Player F, he would have shown them to claim the pot. But Player E wins the pot.

Strategy in Draw Poker— ## Jacks or Better

As with most poker games, the most important strategy is knowing what cards to stay in with, and what hands to fold at the outset.

Even though any hand of jacks or better may open, draw poker is a game of position. Depending upon your position, you open with varying hands. For example, if we were to divide position into early, middle and late, with the first three players having early position, the next three middle and the last two late position, we can see that opening with a pair of jacks in early position is a very weak play.

If any other player stays in and raises, the holder of the jacks would know he is already beaten, and is an underdog to win the pot. The following are guides for opening the pot.

In early position, don't open with less than aces.

In middle position, don't open with less than kings.

In late position you can open with jacks.

The above rules are for very tight players. When there is a larger ante, more than 10% of the highest possible bet, then you can loosen up a little. With a higher ante structure:

- In early position, you can open with kings.
- In middle position, you can open with queens.
- In late position, you can open with jacks.

When you have two small pairs (10s or smaller) you shouldn't open them in early position, and don't even call with them if there are three other players who have already bet. The odds against improving two pairs are 11-1, and you're probably already beaten.

If you hold a pair of kings or aces and are in late position, with only the opener, you can raise with these cards.

With four-straights and four-flushes, don't raise. You have to draw to win, and the odds are approximately 4-1 against you improving your hand.

Study your opposition. See who plays tight and who is weak, and adjust your strategy accordingly. Against tight players, play very conservatively. With weak players, you can be more aggressive and play slightly weaker hands.

34. Draw Poker - Lowball

This is the most popular version of low poker and is sometimes spelled **loball**. Its played at home, in casinos and in the California poker clubs.

Lowball poker is just the opposite of high poker. In this variation of the game, the low hand wins, not the high hand.

The lowest hand in low poker is 5 4 3 2 A, which is known as a *wheel* or *bicycle*. The next best hand is a 6 4 3 2 A, then a 6 5 3 2 A, then a 6 5 4 2 A, and so forth, each hand a little higher than the other.

Lowball—The Wheel

In low poker straights and flushes don't count. You don't have to pay attention to the suits or to the fact that cards may be in consecutive order. What is important is the relative rank of the cards. The most important card in low poker, as it is in high poker, is the ace. But in lowball, it counts as 1 and is always the lowest card in any hand of lowball.

When announcing your holding in low poker, the custom is to call out the two highest cards. For instance, if you held 8 5 4 3 A, you'd call out, "I have an 8 5."

The hands we showed above, the *wheel* and the *6 high* hands, are really and truly the best hands in lowball - premium hands. Any *seven high* hand is very strong. As we get to the *eight high* and hands headed by even higher cards, they lose strength. But remember, any hand of five odd cards will beat any hand containing one pair, because this is the reverse of high poker.

Play of the Game

This game is sometimes played with a joker, known as a **bug**. When it is used in lowball, it can stand for any card the player wants it to be. For example if a player held 7 5 4 3 and Joker, he'd value the Joker as an ace, or 1.

However, many games played at home and in casinos don't have a joker, so we're going to discuss the game without the joker, just using the standard 52 card pack of cards.

There is usually an ante in lowball draw unless there is a blind bettor. Sometimes there is an ante and a blind bettor. For purposes of illustration, let's assume we're playing a $3-$5 game without an ante, but with a blind bettor at a casino in Las Vegas.

To remind you, a $3-$5 game means that all bets before the draw, including raises, are $3 and increments of $3; after the draw, $5 and increments of $5 when raising.

Each player will receive five cards dealt face down one at a time by the dealer, beginning with the player to the button's left and going around the table clockwise. In draw poker, all cards are closed, none of the players see any of the other participant's cards.

After each player has five cards, the player to the button's left being designated as the blind, must make a bet on this round of play, no matter what the value of his hand.

He bets $3. Now, each player in turn, beginning with the blind's left all the way around to the button must either call, raise or fold their cards. No one can check on this round of play. Let's follow a game to see how it works.

Blind	K K Q Q J	Player D.	8 6 5 3 A
Player A.	J 9 9 8 5	Player E.	K 4 3 2 A
Player B.	10 7 5 4 4	Player F.	J 10 10 9 8
Player C.	7 6 5 4 Q	Button	Q 7 7 6 A

The blind must bet $3. Player A and B fold. Player C calls the bet, Player D, with an "8 6 high" raises to $6. Player E calls the raise, Player F and the Button fold. The Blind now folds, and Player C calls the raise by putting in $3 more.

Now the first round of betting is over. Player's C, D and E are remaining in the game. Player C will draw first. He takes one card, discarding his queen. Player D stands **pat**, drawing no cards, satisfied with his hand. Player E draws one card, discarding the king.

Now its up to Player C to go first. He can check on this round and still remain in the game. Here's how the hands now look after the draw.

Player C. 7 6 5 4 J
Player D. 8 6 5 3 A
Player E. 8 4 3 2 A

Player C, whose hand is now pretty bad, checks. Player D bets $5, and Player E raises to $10. Player C folds his cards, and Player D calls the raise by putting in $5 more. All the bets have been made and now we have the showdown. Player E, whose raise was called, shows his "8 4 high." Player D, who has a "8 6 high," concedes the pot to Player E, who wins all the money.

Player E is said to have a **smooth** 8, while Player D had a **rough** 8 high hand. A smooth hand is one where the rest of the cards are very low; a rough one is where they are rather high.

After this game is over, the button will be moved so that the former blind is now the button, while the player to his left, Player A, will now become the blind.

Strategy at Draw Poker - Lowball

As with most other poker games, the important considerations are the cards to stay in with, and our position at the table. If we're the blind, we must stay in with any hand, because we have already bet, and if there are no raises on the first round, we can draw up to five cards to improve our hand. After all, we have nothing to lose. But should there be a raise, and our cards are hopeless, then we fold them, kissing goodbye to the bet we made. Other players will be the blind in turn, and we should assume that a blind bet is no more than a forced ante.

Now, let's go into strategy. We should never stay in the game if we have to draw more than one card. That's the limit. With two cards to draw, we are terrible underdogs, and must be losers in the long run. The way to spot a weak player is to see how many cards he draws. If he draws two, he has little strength.

A pat hand is a hand that will stand by itself without drawing another card to it, and we'll never stay in with pat hands headed by jacks, queens or kings. They're losers. Only in very late position, being the button or next to it, will we hazard a 10 high pat hand, and only to see the blind, without other players in the game.

With a pat hand, we can open (or see the blind bet) with an 8 high hand in the first three positions. In the next three positions we can do the same with a 9 high hand, and only in the last two positions will we do so with a 10 high hand.

When we have a drawing hand, that is, a hand that needs one card to improve it, then our hands have to be a little stronger. In the first three positions at the table, we won't see the blind's bet or open the betting if there's no blind, unless we have a four-card holding of a 7 or less. In the next three positions, an 8 high drawing hand is ok, and in the last two positions, a 9 high drawing hand is sufficient.

When we have pat hands, we can play them more aggressivley. With a 7 high pat hand, we can raise the blind from any position, but with an 8 high pat hand, we can raise from only the last three positions at the table. A 9 high pat hand should be raised against a blind for the last three positions also, but if there has been another player in the game, we just call.

To clarify position once more, the blind is the first position, the button, the last position, and the player to the left of the blind is position 2, the player to his left, position 3, and so forth. Thus, in our illustrative game, Player A was in position 2, while Player F was in seventh position.

When a blind is in the game, and we're in late position with opening hands and there are no other players in the game, we want to raise more aggressively, to force out the blind and win his bet. Don't let the blind stay in to draw cards if you can help it. Get him out, and try to grab his bet if you're in there alone with him.

The games we've discussed here are a fascinating mix of skill, luck and psychology. Using our strategies, you'll take advantage of all these elements to make you a winner!

35. Glossary

Ace—The most valuable card in poker; of highest rank in high poker, and valued as a 1 in lowball.

Ante—Money or chips placed into the pot by players on any betting round.

Bet—Money or chips placed into the pot by players on any betting round.

Betting Round—A round of play in which bets are made.

Bicycle—The best and lowest in lowball, consisting of 5 4 3 2 A, Also called **Wheel**.

Blind, Blind Opener—The player to the left of the dealer or button who must make a mandatory bet on the first betting round.

Bluffing—Betting heavily on a poor hand to give the impression that it has great value.

Board—Cards which are seen by all the players, as in Hold 'Em.

Button—An object resembling a button which is moved around the table clockwise to denote an imaginary dealer.

Buy—See **Draw a Card**.

Buy-In—Money changed into chips prior to play in a casino game.

Call, Call A Bet—Making a bet equal to the previous bet or raise. Also known as **Seeing A Bet**.

Check—Passing the opportunity to bet. Also known as **Pass**.

Check and Raise—Being able to raise after first checking.

Community Cards—In Hold 'Em, cards which can be used by all players to make their best hand.

Deuce—The poker term for the 2.

Draw—The taking of additional cards prior to the second round of betting in draw poker.

Draw A Card—Getting another card prior to any betting round. Also known as **Buy**.

Draw Poker—The closed version of poker.

Flop—The first three open community cards dealt out at one time in Hold 'Em.

Flush—A hand which contains five cards of the same suit.

Fold—Throwing away or discarding one's cards during any betting round.

Four Flush—Having four cards of the same suit.

Four of a Kind—A hand consisting of four cards of the same rank such as 8 8 8 8.

Four Straight—Four cards to a straight.

Full House—A holding of three of a kind plus a pair.

Hand—The five cards a player holds, or the best five cards of his holding which make up his strongest hand.

High Poker—That form of poker in which high hands predominate and win pots.

Hole Card—A card held by the player which is unseen by the other players.

Jacks or Better; Jackpots—High draw poker where a holding of at least a pair of jacks is necessary to open the betting.

Joker—A wild card in lowball which can be used by its holder as any card. Also known as **Bug**.

Kicker—An odd high card, usually an Ace.

Lowball—A poker game in which the low hand wins the pot.

Opener—The player who makes the first bet on any betting round.

Openers—In Jacks or Better, holding at least the pair of jacks after making the first bet.

Pass—See **Check**.

Pat Hand—A hand in draw poker which doesn't need another card drawn to it.

Pot—The amount of money and antes already bet by the players, which amount goes to the winner.

Raise—A bet which is higher than the previous bet.

Rake—The money taken from the pot by the casino as its cut.

Reraise—Making a higher bet than a previous raise.

Rough—In lowball, having high cards which form a hand. For example 9 8 7 5 4 is a rough 9.

See A Bet— See **Call**.

Showdown—Showing of hands after the last bet to determine who is the winner of the pot.

Smooth—In lowball, low cards after the highest card. 9 4 3 2 A is a smooth 9.

Straight—A high poker hand containing five cards of consecutive rank, such as Q J 10 9 8.

Stud Poker—That form of poker where one or more of the player's cards are seen by other players.

Wheel—See **Bicycle**.

Wild Card—A card which can be used by a player to form his best hand by making it into any card he desires.

Six. Keno
36. Introduction

Keno is one of the most popular of the casino games in Nevada, and millions play it every year. The game is fast moving, and for a little bit of money, you can win a great deal, up to $50,000. To win this amount, all that is required is luck and a relatively small bet.

This huge payoff for a small wager makes Keno a very attractive game. You can play the game while in a casino restaurant or while waiting for someone to show up for an appointment. We know of a lucky man who won $12,000 while waiting for his wife to come out of the women's room.

That's the kind of game keno is. Lightning can strike at any moment, and you might be the lucky winner of $50,000.

37. History of Keno

Keno is one of the most ancient of games, and as its name implies, its origins are Oriental. It was invented about two thousand years ago during the Han Dynasty of China, by Cheung Leung, in order to raise money for the army.

It was a great success, and it's popularity has gone on unabated to the present day. Of course, during that long period of time, it underwent a number of changes. Originally it was played in Chinese and contained 120 Chinese characters, drawn from the **Thousand Character Book**, which was written by that great sage, Confucious, and his followers. This work is a classic, and literate Chinese know and study it.

The number of characters was slowly reduced to 90 while the game was played in China, and then, with the great emigrations of Chinese to America, the game was imported, and the characters reduced even further to 80, and today keno is played with the same 80 possibilities, though now the characters have been changed to numbers for simplicity.

Just before the turn of the 20th Century, the game was a very popular one among the Chinese who had settled in several of the big cities, notably San Francisco. It ·was an illegal game, but it was so popular among the Chinese that this didn't seem to matter. It kept growing in popularity.

At this time, the usual ticket was what we'd term a **ten-spot,** that is, ten numbers were selected by the player, and the following were the payoffs. **Catch** refers to the number of characters that were selected by the operator matching the number of characters picked by the players.

Chart 1 19th Century Keno Payoffs	
Catch	**Payoff**
5	2 for 1
6	20 for 1
7	200 for 1
8	1000 for 1
9	1500 for 1
10	3000 for 1

Note the term *2 for 1* which is the payoff for 5 catches. If you bet $1 you'd only get $2 back; your dollar plus a dollar profit. When a payoff is at *2 to 1*, you'd get back your dollar plus two additional dollars.

The game was in the form of a lottery, and the big payoffs possible interested not only the Chinese but other Americans who wanted to take a chance, and in those non-inflationary days, risk a nickel or dime to pick up some good money. But for Americans who couldn't read Chinese, this presented all kinds of difficulties, because it was practically impossible to figure out which characters had caught.

The operators of the game had a big advantage over the players, particularly in the larger payoffs, and so to get Americans to play keno, the game changed from Chinese characters to ordinary numbers, keeping the same format of 80. At this point the keno houses had tickets marked from 1-80, and the numbers, so familiar to Americans, could be easily understood.

In those early days, the numbers were printed on wooden balls, and moved around by hand and then randomly put through a **goose**, a long tube similar to the goose used in keno lounges today. But since hands touched the balls, there was a chance of fixed games. Today, the casinos use air to move ping pong balls imprinted with numbers around as randomly as possible, and then the balls are forced into a goose one by one without anyone touching them. This makes for an honest game, and gives all players the same equal chance to win.

Because the Nevada Gambling Act of 1931, which legalized gambling in the Silver State, expressly forbade lotteries, the casinos introduced the game as *Race Horse Keno*. However, this still created problems, and the race horse aspect of keno was dropped when the US Government passed a law taxing off-track betting. From then on it was plain keno.

The game has grown in popularity year by year, and many old-timers in Las Vegas bemoan the loss of cocktail and entertainment lounges which have turned into keno lounges. But time marches on, and the public's infatuation with the game had to be recognized and taken care of.

Inflation has played a part in the game. In 1963 the payout limit was $25,000 and this stayed in force for a number of years, until 1979 when it was raised to $50,000. And the ticket price has been raised steadily. It has moved up from 60¢ to 70¢ on straight tickets, though today it's hard to buy a keno ticket, particularly on the Las Vegas Strip, for less than $1.

38. Keno Lounge and Employees

The area in which keno is played is called the keno lounge. It consists of a keno counter, behind which sit keno writers, who receive the tickets played by the bettors, mark them and collect money for the game.

In some instances, bettors' tickets are brought to this area by **keno runners**. These house employees, usually women, pick up tickets from people who want to play the next game, but can't get to the keno lounge. This includes bettors at table games, and people who are in the various restaurants or other parts of the casino. In this way, through the use of keno runners, players in a casino, no matter where they are, can usually play keno without having to go to the keno lounge.

Not only do the keno writers collect bets; they also make the payoffs on winning tickets. Behind the keno writers is the operator who calls the game. He sits on an elevated seat and starts the game by pressing a button which automatically mixes the ping pong balls. They are in a large transparent bowl, and are stirred at random by the insertion of air forced into the bowl, which in turn forces the balls, one by one, into one of two transparent gooses, which are long tubes, each of which hold ten balls.

After the game commences, as each numbered ball is pushed into a goose, the operator calls that number aloud, and then that number is marked electrically on a keno board. This board holds all the 80 numbers, and lights up each number as it is called. After twenty numbers have been called, the game is over. From these twenty numbers, each player will examine his or her ticket to see if he or she has *caught* enough numbers to collect some money.

Keno boards are located throughout the casino and adjacent areas, such as restaurants and coffee shops, so that players, no matter where they are when playing the game, can see if they won or lost.

The keno lounge is made up of rows of seats, each with an armrest. On each armrest is a box holding the crayons and keno blanks which are used to play the game.

While in the keno lounge, a player can order beverages from waitresses who constantly service the area. These beverages are free to active keno players, who usually tip, or toke the waitresses when they receive their complimentary drinks.

39. How to Play Keno

Let's assume you're at the keno lounge and want to play a game. The first thing you'll notice is that the board will be lit by twenty numbers from the previous game. At the bottom of the board there will be another figure, indicating the number of the previous game. For instance, if the bottom number is 236, game 236 has just been played, and the next game will be game 237. The number will be changed to 237 when all the 20 numbers have been turned off, indicating that a new sequence of numbers is about to be called for game 237. Once the board is empty of printed numbers, it's too late to make a keno bet. The next game is on.

But while the board is filled with 20 lit numbers, bets can be made for the next game. To do this, the player must first pick up a blank ticket, also know as a **blank**, and fill it in. He or she should not only **"X" out** the numbers he selects, which may be from 1 to

15 spots, but also the amount to be bet, and the number of spots selected. First, let's look at a keno blank.

Keno Blank

This blank is from a very popular gambing casino in downtown Las Vegas. Notice that between the top and bottom row of numbers is a statement *Keno LIMIT $50,000 To aggregate players each game.*

This means that the most the casino will pay out for any game of keno is $50,000. In the unlikely event that two players will be entitled to $50,000 for one game's payoff, they will each get $25,000. That's the rule because of the gambling commission laws. But don't worry about that. It is very unlikely that anyone will win $50,000, let along two players winning that amount and having to split it.

Next notice that there's a rectangular box in the upper right hand corner marked *Mark Price Here.* The player should put in that box the amount he wants to bet. If it's $1, then $1 should be put into the box. But leave out the dollar ($) or cents (¢) sign when doing this.

To the right of the numbers is another long blank space. In this space, the bettor should put the total spots selected. If two numbers are selected, the ticket is known as a **two-spot** ticket. A player can select up to fifteen spots on a straight ticket.

The numbers selected should be **"X"ed out** using the crayon the casino has available to all keno bettors. After you've Xed out the numbers, add up the spots selected, and put this number to the right of the ticket. Then put in the amount you wish to bet in the price box on the right hand top corner of the ticket.

When that's done, bring the ticket to the keno writer. If you're in the keno lounge you can go directly to the keno writer. If you're not in the lounge, you'd give the keno ticket and the bet to a runner.

The following is a filled-in ticket. It is known as an **original** or **master** ticket. It is a **five-spot straight ticket**, since five numbers were selected, and it is being played for $1.

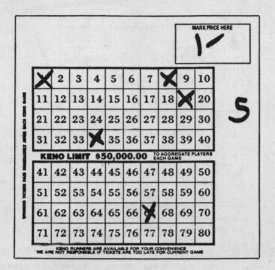

Five-Spot Original Ticket

With this ticket in hand, you go to the keno writer, and pay the writer a dollar to play the next game. He or she will retain the master and give you back a **duplicate** ticket, which you hold onto till the game is over. A duplicate ticket of the original we showed will look like this:

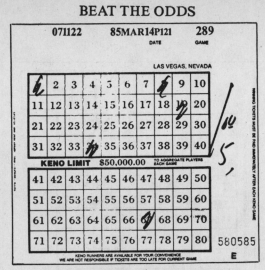

Five-Spot Duplicate ticket

This duplicate shows a few things that weren't on the original blank. There's the date and time the ticket way played, and the game number, which is 289. There's also another code number. All these are printed on duplicates to prevent collusion and cheating and to protect the players and the casino.

Note also at this time someting printed down the right side of the ticket. *"Winning tickets must be paid immediately after each keno game."* If you're entitled to a payoff, you **must** present your duplicate ticket to the writer or runner before the next game is called: otherwise you'll forfeit your winnings. This rule is in effect to prevent the keno game from being called a lottery; where winning tickets can be collected at any time. This is important; don't forget to collect your winnings before the next game is called, or you won't collect anything.

The ticket just played is known as a **five-spot**, since five numbers were selected. It's a straight ticket because it was played only one way, and if enough numbers were called by the operator there would be a payoff.

In order to collect and win with this 5-spot ticket, at least three numbers would have to catch. The payoff possibilities at this downtown casino are as follows:

Chart 2	
A Five Spot Payoff	
Winning Spots	**Payoff**
3	1.00
4	14.00
5	720.00

That's for a $1 ticket. If the player played a $2 ticket, the payoffs would be exactly double, and for a $5 ticket, they'd be five times the $1 payoff. The player doesn't get better odds playing for more money; all he does is risk more to collect more.

How does the player know how much he will collect and how many numbers he or she must catch to win some money? There are small booklets available at each seat in the keno lounge and at each table in the casino restaurant which show the payoffs and the bets allowed. These are also known as **rate cards**.

A sample rate card, showing all payoffs and bets available, as well as the total numbers one must catch to win anything, is shown next.

Chart 3
Rate Card: 1-15 Spots, $1 Bet

MARK 1 SPOT

Winning Spots	$1.00 Ticket Pays	$3.00 Ticket Pays	$5.00 Ticket Pays	$1.40 Ticket Pays
1	3.00	9.00	15.00	4.20

MARK 2 SPOTS

Winning Spots	$1.00 Ticket Pays	$3.00 Ticket Pays	$5.00 Ticket Pays	$1.40 Ticket Pays
2	12.00	36.00	60.00	17.00

MARK 3 SPOTS

Winning Spots	$1.00 Ticket Pays	$3.00 Ticket Pays	$5.00 Ticket Pays	$1.40 Ticket Pays
2	1.00	3.00	5.00	1.40
3	42.00	126.00	210.00	60.00

MARK 4 SPOTS

Winning Spots	$1.00 Ticket Pays	$3.00 Ticket Pays	$5.00 Ticket Pays	$1.40 Ticket Pays
2	1.00	3.00	5.00	1.40
3	4.00	12.00	20.00	5.40
4	112.00	336.00	560.00	160.00

MARK 5 SPOTS

Winning Spots	$1.00 Ticket Pays	$3.00 Ticket Pays	$5.00 Ticket Pays	$1.40 Ticket Pays
3	1.00	3.00	5.00	2.40
4	14.00	42.00	70.00	30.00
5	720.00	2,160.00	3,600.00	680.00

MARK 13 SPOTS

Winning Spots	$1.00 Ticket Pays	$3.00 Ticket Pays	$5.00 Ticket Pays	$1.40 Ticket Pays
6	1.00	3.00	5.00	2.40
7	16.00	48.00	80.00	24.00
8	80.00	240.00	400.00	100.00
9	720.00	2,160.00	3,800.00	950.00
10	4,000.00	12,000.00	20,000.00	5,000.00
11	8,000.00	24,000.00	40,000.00	9,000.00
12	25,000.00	50,000.00	50,000.00	20,000.00
13	36,000.00	50,000.00	50,000.00	50,000.00

MARK 14 SPOTS

Winning Spots	$1.00 Ticket Pays	$3.00 Ticket Pays	$5.00 Ticket Pays	$1.40 Ticket Pays
6	1.00	3.00	5.00	4.40
7	10.00	30.00	50.00	11.00
8	40.00	120.00	200.00	44.00
9	320.00	960.00	1,600.00	350.00
10	1,000.00	3,000.00	5,000.00	1,000.00
11	3,200.00	9,600.00	16,000.00	4,000.00
12	16,000.00	48,000.00	50,000.00	15,000.00
13	25,000.00	50,000.00	50,000.00	30,000.00
14	40,000.00	50,000.00	50,000.00	50,000.00

MARK 15 SPOTS

Winning Spots	$1.00 Ticket Pays	$3.00 Ticket Pays	$5.00 Ticket Pays	$1.40 Ticket Pays
6				2.00
7	8.00	24.00	40.00	10.00
8	28.00	84.00	140.00	30.00
9	132.00	396.00	660.00	150.00
10	300.00	900.00	1,500.00	400.00
11	2,600.00	7,800.00	13,000.00	3,000.00
12	8,000.00	24,000.00	40,000.00	10,000.00
13	25,000.00	50,000.00	50,000.00	30,000.00
14	32,000.00	50,000.00	50,000.00	40,000.00
15	40,000.00	50,000.00	50,000.00	50,000.00

MARK 6 SPOTS

Winning Spots	$1.00 Ticket Pays	$3.00 Ticket Pays	$5.00 Ticket Pays	$1.40 Ticket Pays
3	1.00	3.00	5.00	1.20
4	4.00	12.00	20.00	6.60
5	88.00	264.00	440.00	120.00
6	1,480.00	4,440.00	7,400.00	2,200.00

MARK 7 SPOTS

Winning Spots	$1.00 Ticket Pays	$3.00 Ticket Pays	$5.00 Ticket Pays	$1.40 Ticket Pays
3				60
4	1.00	3.00	5.00	2.40
5	20.00	60.00	100.00	30.00
6	380.00	1,140.00	1,900.00	460.00
7	8,000.00	24,000.00	40,000.00	7,000.00

MARK 8 SPOTS

Winning Spots	$1.00 Ticket Pays	$3.00 Ticket Pays	$5.00 Ticket Pays	$1.40 Ticket Pays
5	9.00	27.00	45.00	12.00
6	80.00	240.00	400.00	120.00
7	1,480.00	4,440.00	7,400.00	2,300.00
8	25,000.00	50,000.00	50,000.00	25,000.00

MARK 9 SPOTS

Winning Spots	$1.00 Ticket Pays	$3.00 Ticket Pays	$5.00 Ticket Pays	$1.40 Ticket Pays
4				60
5	4.00	12.00	20.00	4.60
6	44.00	132.00	220.00	60.00
7	300.00	900.00	1,500.00	400.00
8	4,000.00	12,000.00	20,000.00	5,600.00
9	25,000.00	50,000.00	50,000.00	25,000.00

MARK 10 SPOTS

Winning Spots	$1.00 Ticket Pays	$3.00 Ticket Pays	$5.00 Ticket Pays	$1.40 Ticket Pays
5	2.00	6.00	10.00	2.80
6	20.00	60.00	100.00	28.00
7	136.00	408.00	680.00	196.00
8	960.00	2,880.00	4,800.00	1,400.00
9	4,000.00	12,000.00	20,000.00	5,320.00
10	25,000.00	50,000.00	50,000.00	25,000.00

MARK 11 SPOTS

Winning Spots	$1.00 Ticket Pays	$3.00 Ticket Pays	$5.00 Ticket Pays	$1.40 Ticket Pays
5	1.00	3.00	5.00	1.20
6	8.00	24.00	40.00	12.00
7	72.00	216.00	360.00	100.00
8	360.00	1,080.00	1,800.00	500.00
9	1,800.00	5,400.00	9,000.00	2,400.00
10	12,000.00	36,000.00	50,000.00	15,000.00
11	28,000.00	50,000.00	50,000.00	40,000.00

MARK 12 SPOTS

Winning Spots	$1.00 Ticket Pays	$3.00 Ticket Pays	$5.00 Ticket Pays	$1.40 Ticket Pays
5				1.20
6	5.00	15.00	25.00	6.00
7	32.00	96.00	160.00	40.00
8	240.00	720.00	1,200.00	300.00
9	600.00	1,800.00	3,000.00	800.00
10	1,480.00	4,440.00	7,400.00	2,000.00
11	12,000.00	36,000.00	50,000.00	10,000.00
12	36,000.00	50,000.00	50,000.00	50,000.00

Keno runners are available for your convenience. Since they must transport your tickets to the main counter for validation, please have the tickets ready as early as possible. We cannot accept responsibility if tickets are too late for the current game.

Chart 4
Rate Card: 1-15 Spots, $1.40 Bet

MARK 1 SPOT

Catch	Play 1.40	Play 3.50	Play 7.00
1 Pays	4.20	10.50	21.00

MARK 2 SPOTS

Catch	Play 1.40	Play 3.50	Play 7.00
2 Pays	17.00	42.50	85.00

MARK 3 SPOTS

Catch	Play 1.40	Play 3.50	Play 7.00
2 Pays	1.40	3.50	7.00
3 Pays	60.00	150.00	300.00

MARK 4 SPOTS

Catch	Play 1.40	Play 3.50	Play 7.00
2 Pays	1.40	3.50	7.00
3 Pays	5.40	13.50	27.00
4 Pays	160.00	400.00	800.00

MARK 5 SPOTS

Catch	Play 1.40	Play 3.50	Play 7.00
3 Pays	2.40	6.00	12.00
4 Pays	30.00	75.00	150.00
5 Pays	680.00	1,700.00	3,400.00

MARK 6 SPOTS

Catch	Play 1.40	Play 3.50	Play 7.00
3 Pays	1.20	3.00	6.00
4 Pays	6.60	16.50	33.00
5 Pays	120.00	300.00	600.00
6 Pays	2,200.00	5,500.00	11,000.00

MARK 7 SPOTS

Catch	Play 1.40	Play 3.50	Play 7.00
3 Pays	.60	1.50	3.00
4 Pays	2.40	6.00	12.00
5 Pays	30.00	75.00	150.00
6 Pays	460.00	1,150.00	2,300.00
7 Pays	7,000.00	17,500.00	35,000.00

MARK 8 SPOTS

Catch	Play 1.40	Play 3.50	Play 7.00
5 Pays	12.00	30.00	60.00
6 Pays	120.00	300.00	600.00
7 Pays	2,300.00	5,750.00	11,500.00
8 Pays	25,000.00	50,000.00	50,000.00

MARK 9 SPOTS

Catch	Play 1.40	Play 3.50	Play 7.00
4 Pays	.60	1.50	3.00
5 Pays	4.60	11.50	23.00
6 Pays	60.00	150.00	300.00
7 Pays	400.00	1,000.00	2,000.00
8 Pays	5,600.00	14,000.00	26,000.00
9 Pays	25,000.00	50,000.00	50,000.00

MARK 10 SPOTS

Catch	Play 1.40	Play 3.50	Play 7.00
5 Pays	2.80	7.00	14.00
6 Pays	28.00	70.00	140.00
7 Pays	196.00	490.00	980.00
8 Pays	1,400.00	3,500.00	7,000.00
9 Pays	5,320.00	13,300.00	26,600.00
10 Pays	25,000.00	50,000.00	50,000.00

MARK 11 SPOTS

Catch	Play 1.40	Play 3.50	Play 7.00
5 Pays	1.20	3.00	6.00
6 Pays	12.00	30.00	60.00
7 Pays	100.00	250.00	500.00
8 Pays	500.00	1,250.00	2,500.00
9 Pays	2,400.00	6,000.00	12,000.00
10 Pays	15,000.00	37,500.00	50,000.00
11 Pays	25,000.00	50,000.00	50,000.00

MARK 12 SPOTS

Catch	Play 1.40	Play 3.50	Play 7.00
6 Pays	1.20	3.00	6.00
7 Pays	6.00	15.00	30.00
8 Pays	40.00	100.00	200.00
9 Pays	300.00	750.00	1,500.00
10 Pays	800.00	2,000.00	4,000.00
11 Pays	2,000.00	5,000.00	10,000.00
12 Pays	10,000.00	25,000.00	50,000.00

MARK 13 SPOTS

Catch	Play 1.40	Play 3.50	Play 7.00
6 Pays	2.40	6.00	12.00
7 Pays	24.00	60.00	120.00
8 Pays	100.00	250.00	500.00
9 Pays	950.00	2,375.00	4,750.00
10 Pays	5,000.00	12,500.00	25,000.00
11 Pays	9,000.00	22,500.00	45,000.00
12 Pays	20,000.00	50,000.00	50,000.00
13 Pays	50,000.00	50,000.00	50,000.00

MARK 14 SPOTS

Catch	Play 1.40	Play 3.50	Play 7.00
6 Pays	4.40	11.00	22.00
7 Pays	11.00	27.50	55.00
8 Pays	44.00	110.00	220.00
9 Pays	350.00	875.00	1,750.00
10 Pays	1,000.00	2,500.00	5,000.00
11 Pays	4,000.00	10,000.00	20,000.00
12 Pays	15,000.00	37,500.00	50,000.00
13 Pays	30,000.00	50,000.00	50,000.00
14 Pays	50,000.00	50,000.00	50,000.00

MARK 15 SPOTS

Catch	Play 1.40	Play 3.50	Play 7.00
6 Pays	2.00	5.00	10.00
7 Pays	10.00	25.00	50.00
8 Pays	30.00	75.00	150.00
9 Pays	150.00	375.00	750.00
10 Pays	400.00	1,000.00	2,000.00
11 Pays	3,000.00	7,500.00	15,000.00
12 Pays	10,000.00	25,000.00	50,000.00
13 Pays	30,000.00	50,000.00	50,000.00
14 Pays	40,000.00	50,000.00	50,000.00
15 Pays	50,000.00	50,000.00	50,000.00

Regulations require that all winning tickets must be collected immediately after each game.

Keno runners are for your convenience. Mark your tickets early to avoid missing a game. We are not responsible if tickets arrive too late for game played.

$50,000.00 LIMIT EACH GAME
AGGREGATE PAYOFF

70¢ Minimum Play

In most downtown Las Vegas casinos, the minimum bet is 70¢. The next rate card shows payoffs for $1.40 bet. When betting 70¢, simply divide the payoff by 2.

And that's the procedure for playing keno. You mark your ticket by putting X's in crayon on the numbers you select, you write the price of the ticket and total number of spots selected and bring it to the keno writer.

If you want to use a keno runner, then you give the runner the money necessary to play the ticket so marked, and you will receive back a duplicate ticket from her. If there's a payoff, you can give her the winning ticket. She'll collect the winnings for you.

Remember again, and this is very important. If you have a winning ticket, make certain you collect before the next game is called; otherwise you forfeit the payoff.

In order to verify whether or not you won any money for a particular game, the keno writer will place a **punch-out** ticket over your ticket, to see how many numbers have caught. A punch-out ticket contains, as the name implies, punch-outs of the numbers called. At the same time that the operator calls each number selected, that same number is punched out automatically.

If in doubt about whether or not you've won, you can request the punch-out ticket and place your ticket under it. The following is a punch-out ticket from a Strip hotel in Las Vegas.

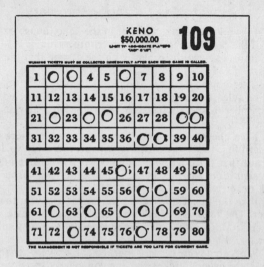

Punch-Out Ticket

Replaying the Ticket

Many players have favorite numbers they bet on to the exclusion of other numbers. They may select a group of numbers and keep playing those same numbers all day long. If that's the case, it's not necessary to keep writing new tickets.

When you wish to replay a ticket, you simply hand in the duplicate ticket you've been issued by the keno writer, and this now becomes the original, and you're given a new duplicate. You can do this indefinitely, until you get tired of the numbers, or you finally hit it big.

Chart 5
How to Play Keno – Summary

1. Take a keno blank, whether in the keno lounge or in any area of the casino where keno runners are available, and X out the numbers you wish to play with the crayon that the casino offers.

2. After you've Xed out the numbers, add them up. There must be at least 1 and no more than 15 numbers selected. Place this number of spots selected in the right hand margin of the ticket.

3. Then choose the amount you want to bet, checking the rate card first to see the possible payoffs. After you've decided this, put that price without using either a dollar sign ($) or a cents sign (¢) in the box in the upper right hand corner of the blank ticket.

4. Take the ticket up to the keno writer or give it to a keno runner. The keno writer will give you back a duplicate, as will the keno runner, after you pay the money necessary to play the ticket.

5. Verify that your ticket is marked correctly. When there's a dispute, the original ticket, the one you marked, predominates.

6. Watch the board to see if you've caught enough numbers for a payoff. If you have, then go up immediately, before the next game is called, and collect your payoff.

If you use a keno runner, have her collect for you by giving her the ticket and telling her there's money to be collected. She'll do it for you. It is customary to toke the runner in this event, or the keno writer if you've collected a substantial amount.

7. If in doubt about winning, either check the punch-out ticket, or have the keno writer do it for you. He'll be happy to accomodate you.

8. You're not limited to playing one ticket. You can play several if you want, at one time, as long as you follow the procedure of marking them correctly.

9. You can replay your ticket, by either giving the duplicate to the keno writer, or handing it to the keno runner and stating that you wish to replay the ticket.

10. Don't fold or mutilate your ticket or mark it in any way. It's a very valuable commodity, especially if you catch some winning numbers.

40. Straight Tickets

In our discussion concering the writing of keno tickets, we showed how a straight ticket should be written and bet upon. A straight ticket is the most common kind of ticket, which can be marked up from 1 to 15 numbers and played for either the minimum amount, usually 70¢ in downtown Las Vegas, Reno and Late Tahoe, or for $1 or $2 minimum in the fancier Strip hotels.

When playing straight tickets, you can play either for the minimum for multiples of the minimum. However, if you're aiming to win $50,000, you don't have to bet too much over the minimum. For example, if you're playing a 12-spot (12 numbers), a $1.40 bet entitles you to $50,000 if you hit all the numbers. And when playing 13, 14 and 15 spot tickets, the same bet will get you $50,000.

However, with an 8-9-10 or 11 spot, you'd have to bet $3.50 to win $50,000, and the amount bet increases dramatically when playing smaller spot tickets. If you play a 6-spot, for example, it would take about $32.20 to win the $50,000.

Most beginning players, and even experienced players, prefer the straight tickets. They're simple to play, and the payoffs are simple to calculate. However, these aren't the only tickets that can be written, and some others offer a variety of payoffs and possibilities, making keno even more interesting to play.

41. Split Tickets

A **split ticket** allows a player to write two or more tickets in one, splitting the numbers by either circling them or drawing a line between them. When writing a split ticket, the player is limited in that the numbers in one group can't be duplicated in the other group. They must be kept separate. But a player may mark 1 to 15 numbers in each group. The following are two split tickets, one separated by circling one group, and the other by drawing a line.

Before we examine these tickets, remember that you're not limited to two games at one time. If you want to, you can split the ticket three or more ways, as long as there are sufficient numbers that can't be duplicated. For example, if you played two-spots you could split the ticket 40 ways, but this kind of splitting isn't recommended.

One final note. Some casinos will allow a player to bet on split tickets at a reduced rate, usually half of the minimum. Thus, if a player split a ticket into four tickets, where the minimum was $1, he could play for $2, each split ticket worth 50¢. However, if he catches good, then the payoff will be one-half of what the rate card shows for $1.

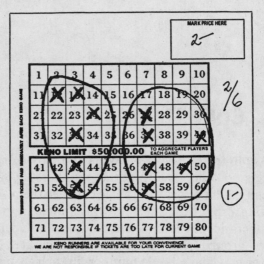

Split Ticket - Circled Numbers

The above split ticket is made up of two 6-spots, each played for $1. The player should mark the total price in the upper right hand box, then mark 2/6 to show that two separate six-spot straight tickets are being played as a split ticket. Then he should circle at the bottom margin the price for each individual split ticket.

To be doubly safe, inform the keno writer that this is a split ticket. The next split ticket is of 5-spots, the two parts separated by a line.

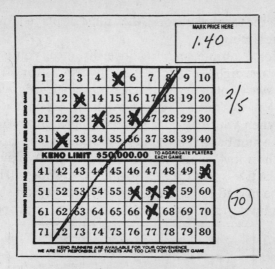

Split Ticket - Line Separated

When playing a split ticket, it's important to remember that each split part is played as a separate ticket, so, if you play two six-spots and need to catch three numbers for a payoff, you'll have to catch those three on one of the split parts. You can't take two numbers from one part and one from the other for a payoff.

When playing split tickets, you don't have to have equal groups. You might divide the ticket, that is, split it, so that you're playing two 5-spots, one eight-spot and three two-spots, for example. On the margin you'd write 1/8, 2/5 and 3/2, showing that you're playing one eight-spot, two five-spots and three two-spots. You can play them for different amounts of money, but if you're playing at least two with the same spot total, they must be played for the same amount.

For example, in the above instance, you could play the eight-spot for $1, the five-spots for $2 and the two-spots for 70¢ each. In other words, you'd have to lay out $7.10 to play the ticket that way.

When you play split tickets, all groupings of the same number of spots must be for the same amount. In the above example, for instance, if you play one of the five-spots for $2, the other five-spot will have to be played for $2 also. The following ticket shows just how this is done, marking the ticket properly.

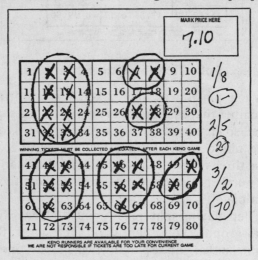

Split Ticket - Six Groups

42. Way Tickets

A **way ticket** gives the player more versatility than a split ticket. A way ticket must have at least three groups of **equal amounts** of numbers to qualify as such. These equal groups combine with other equal groups to form several straight ticket combinations.

Unlike the straight ticket, if you catch three numbers from one group and two from another, you have a winner, because you combine here, rather than separate the individual groups. Way tickets can sometimes lead to big payoffs, because it's possible to win more than one way.

Let's examine a simple way ticket to see how this is accomplished. This ticket will contain three four-spots, but will not be written as a three four-spot ticket, which would be the case with a split ticket, but as a three eight-spot, because with a way ticket, we combine, rather than separate the three groups.

First, let's look at the ticket for easier clarification.

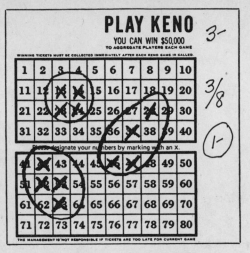

Way Ticket - Three 8-Spots

The ticket shows three separate equal groups which combine together to form three eight-spots. Here's how it's done. If we assume that group A consists of 13, 14, 23, and 24; group B consists of 42, 52, 53, and 63; and group C consists of 28, 37, 46, and 47, these are the possible combining situations; AB, AC and BC, three in all. Thus, from three four-spots, we can make three eight-spots. Then we must play them all at the same rate. On the Strip, there'd be a minimum of $1 per way. Thus our ticket would be for $3.

With an eight-spot, it's necessary to hit or catch at least 5 numbers to get a payoff. Since this kind of ticket is a little more complicated, we suggest you give the ticket to the keno writer after the game is called, just to verify the possibility of winning if you're in doubt.

43. Combination Tickets

A **combination ticket** is a bit more complicated
and much more versatile than either a split or way
ticket. It gives a player all kinds of chances to win
playing but one ticket. Let's look at a ticket with
three equal groups of four-spots to see how this can
be played as a combination ticket.

Combination Ticket - Four Ways

What we've done is set up a combination ticket with three eight-spots and one twelve-spot. The twelve-spot is made by combining the three four-spots. Each is played for $1 a way, for a total of $4.

We can go even farther with this same ticket.

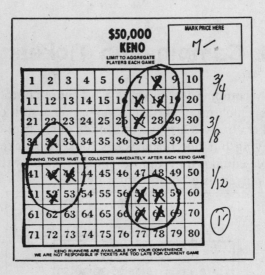

Combination Ticket - Seven Ways

Now we've extended the ticket so that we are playing three four-spots, three eight-spots and one twelve-spot, each for a dollar for a total of $7. We have all kinds of ways to win with this ticket.

Often combination tickets aren't played with equal groupings. The following is a good example of a versatile combination ticket containing three unequal groups of numbers.

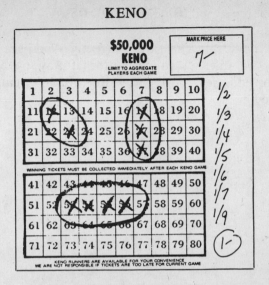

Combination Ticket - Unequal Groupings

With the above ticket, we have conditioned the ticket so that we play seven different combinations with one ticket. We have unequal groups of two, three, and four-spots. They combine for these seven types of possible tickets. Played at $1 per way, these seven ways would cost $7 to play.

Some casinos would allow you to play at cheaper prices per way. Speak to the keno writer before writing any kinds of tickets but straight tickets, and find out the cheapest possible rates allowed. As we can see, it can become quite expensive to play a game of keno if we have to pay high rates and have a number of ways going for us.

If you write a very complicated combination ticket, then go over it carefully with the keno writer.

making certain it's written correctly. And because it may be difficult to determine if any payoff is involved, check with the writer after the game is called.

44. King Ticket

A **king ticket** may be defined as any ticket in which there appears a single circled number. This single number is the **king**, and is not played alone, but is combined with other numbers to form various ways. Let's look at a sample king ticket.

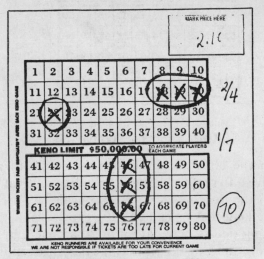

King Ticket - Three Ways

In the above ticket, the number *"22"* was king, and was used in combination with each three-spot separately to form two four-spots, and then in combination with both three-spots to form one seven-spot. This is a fairly simple king ticket. The next one is a bit more complicated.

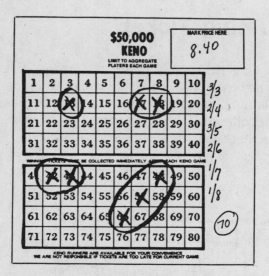

King Ticket - Twelve Ways

In the above example, we were able to make twelve different ways out of one ticket. Even at 70¢ a way, the tickets cost $8.40. So again, we see that these keno tickets can become expensive.

King tickets may have more than one king, and there are all king tickets that can be written. But they should be carefully studied, because of their complex nature. And always consult with a keno writer when you're not sure of how to write the ticket, or not sure if you've gotten a payoff. They'll be happy to help, and don't forget to toke them for their aid.

45. Special Tickets

Some casinos will have **special tickets**, with different rate structures. The following are examples of these. These special tickets vary from casino to casino, and may be changed from time to time.

When writing a special ticket, the casinos require that the player mark a "sp" for special on the ticket, to differentiate it from the normal ticket paid according to the casino keno rate book.

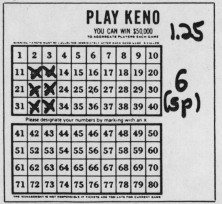

Six-Spot Special Ticket

Chart 6
Special Tickets

$1.25 Super Specials!!

– 6 SPOT –

4 OUT OF 6 PAYS	1.00
5 OUT OF 6 PAYS	25.00
6 OUT OF 6 PAYS	2000.00

– 7 SPOT –

5 OUT OF 7 PAYS	10.00
6 OUT OF 7 PAYS	180.00
7 OUT OF 7 PAYS	7000.00

– 8 SPOT –

6 OUT OF 8 PAYS	30.00
7 OUT OF 8 PAYS	900.00
8 OUT OF 8 PAYS	25,000.00

YOU CAN PLAY AS MANY TICKETS
ON EACH GAME AS YOU WISH

Mark One Spot

CATCH	$2.00 Ticket Pays	$3.00 Ticket Pays	$5.00 Ticket Pays	$10.00 Ticket Pays
1	6.00	9.00	15.00	30.00

Mark Two Spot

CATCH	$2.00 Ticket Pays	$3.00 Ticket Pays	$5.00 Ticket Pays	$10.00 Ticket Pays
2	24.00	36.00	60.00	120.00

Mark Three Spot

CATCH	$2.00 Ticket Pays	$3.00 Ticket Pays	$5.00 Ticket Pays	$10.00 Ticket Pays
2	2.00	3.00	5.00	10.00
3	84.00	126.00	210.00	420.00

SPECIAL THREE SPOT

CATCH	$3.00 Ticket Pays	$5.00 Ticket Pays	$9.00 Ticket Pays
3	150.00	250.00	450.00

IT IS THE CUSTOMERS
RESPONSIBILITY TO WRITE "SP" FOR
SPECIAL ON THE ORIGINAL TICKET.

Mark Four Spot

CATCH	$2.00 Ticket Pays	$3.00 Ticket Pays	$5.00 Ticket Pays	$10.00 Ticket Pays
2	2.00	3.00	5.00	10.00
3	8.00	12.00	20.00	40.00
4	224.00	336.00	560.00	1,120.00

$3.00 MINIMUM ON SPECIAL TICKETS

SPECIAL FOUR SPOT

CATCH	$3.00 Ticket Pays	$5.00 Ticket Pays	$9.00 Ticket Pays	$20.00 Ticket Pays
3	15.00	25.00	45.00	100.00
4	480.00	800.00	1,440.00	3,200.00

46. Casino Advantage in Keno

The calculations to be made in keno are rather complex, and the permutations and combinations run into the millions. The advantage however, is never less than 25% and runs up to about 35%.

The odds are strongly against the player, but this is to be expected where the payoff is so huge and the risk so small.

But no matter what the special ticket is, no matter what exotic payoffs are offered by the casino, expect to face these odds when playing keno.

47. Taxes on Keno Winnings

All gambling wins are taxable, and losses from gambling may be deducted from gambling winnings. The IRS requires the casino to have a winner of at least $1,500 net identify himself or herself adequately by showing a driver's license, credit card or social security card. Then that person's winnings will be reported to the IRS, and the winner should report those winnings on his or her income tax.

Nothing will be deducted from the winning amount unless the person winning is a non-resident alien. Then 30% will be withheld from the winning amount and sent by the casino directly to the IRS. A Canadian citizen will have 15% taken out of the winning amount.

When playing keno, have some identification with you, so that, in the event you do win a big amount, you can easily collect by showing the proper verifiable information and identification.

48. Playing Strategy for Keno

This game should not be played seriously for big money. There are many other games the casino offers with better odds for the player. But, in order to take advantage of the game and to have the chance to win big money, we suggest that a player attempt to win as much as possible.

Avoid all games under 7-spots. With a $1 bet, you can win $18,000 in an eight-spot game, $20,000 in a nine-spot game, $25,000 in a ten-spot game. Check on the casinos; some pay more than others. In some casinos, a $1 bet on a 14-spot game will pay $25,000; another will pay $40,000 if you catch all the numbers.

Playing for $1.40, you'll get $50,000 if you catch all the numbers on any 12, 13, 14, or 15-spot game in downtown Las Vegas.

If you want to play keno, it's better to risk $1.40 downtown than $2 on the Strip for the same payoff. Check the rate cards in the casinos you enter, by going to the keno lounge and looking at them carefully. Shop around; don't throw away money. A 60¢ savings on each ticket adds up, because the games move right along

If you have favorite numbers, then it's best to stick to them. There's nothing worse than going off a set of numbers, only to watch them catch the next game without a payoff for you. But don't be oblivious of the numbers that come up frequently. There may be a bias in the ping-pong balls, or the way they're blown around.

Some players pick numbers that haven't come up for a long time; others pick those that frequently catch. Keno is a game of chance; you take your chances when you pick numbers, for they'll be coming up in a random sequence.

But go for the big money, no matter what numbers you want to play. That's where the real enjoyment of keno comes in; the possibility of winning that $50,000. Good luck.

49. Glossary

Blank, Blank Ticket—A ticket marked with from 1-80 numbers not yet filled in by the player.

Board, Keno Board—An electrical setup showing the 80 numbers of keno in various parts of the casino, with the 20 numbers selected lit up when they are called.

Bowl—The cage that holds the marked ping-pong balls used in keno.

Caller—The casino employee who operates the blower and calls out the numbers selected.

Catch—A number selected by a player which has been called by the operator of the game.

Combination Ticket—A versatile ticket that allows groups of numbers to combine with other groups.

Conditioning—The way a player decides to play his ticket written as fractions, such as 2/8 meaning two eight-spots.

Draw—The selecting of a numbered ball into the goose at random.

Duplicate Ticket—The ticket marked in india ink by the keno writer and returned to the player.

Goose—Each of two transparent tubes holding ten balls apiece after they've been forced in by a hot air blower.

Group—Several numbers separated by other numbers through the use of a circle or line.

Keno Lounge—The area in which the game of keno is played, called and operated.

Keno Runner—A casino employee who collects players' tickets and bets, brings them to the keno writer, and then collects payoffs if there is a winning ticket.

Keno Writer—The casino employee who collects the player's bet, writes the duplicate and pays off the winners.

King, King Number—A single separate number which combines with other groups of numbers to make a versatile ticket.

Original Ticket—The ticket filled out by the player and presented to the keno writer for a duplicate ticket.

Punch-Outs—Also known as a draw ticket. This shows the selected 20 numbers for any game punched out on a keno blank.

Rate Card—The booklet issued by a casino showing bets and payoffs on various spots selected by the player.

Special Tickets—Tickets other than the normal ones in the casino rate book, with special prices and payoffs.

Split Ticket—A ticket with two or more groups of numbers played separately.

Spot, Spots—These indicate the number of choices the player selects on a ticket. If he or she selects five numbers, it's a five-spot ticket.

Straight Ticket—A ticket in which one to fifteen numbers are selected without combinations of any kind.

Way Ticket—A ticket with at least three different groups of numbers combining in various ways.

Writer—See **Keno Writer**.

Seven. Slots

50. Introduction to Slots

This book will show you all you need to know to win money at slots. You'll learn which casinos to play in, what machines to play, how to leave a winner.

But that's not all you'll learn. There's a history of the slot machine and the various machines made over the years. There's inside information on how casinos set their slots, how the odds are figured, how slots are set up in a casino—some to pay off big, others tight with their rewards.

By the time you finish this book, you'll be informed, entertained, and, best of all, you'll be a winner.

Liberty Bells

51. History of Slots

The invention of the slot machine is credited to a Bavarian immigrant, Charles Fey, who, while working as a mechanic in San Francisco, at the end of the 19th century, perfected a gambling device which was very similar to the slots we're familiar with today.

The machines invented by Fey began to appear in bars and saloons around the Bay Area in the 1890s, and the payoffs were supposedly in free drinks if the correct symbols were lined up. But one can only drink so much, and, as the players grew a little more sophisticated, they demanded and got payoffs in coins.

The symbols used on these first machines, which were known as Liberty Bells, were of playing card suits: diamonds, hearts, clubs and spades. But there were other symbols as well, ten symbols on each reel, and since there were three reels, there were 1,000 possible combinations that could be spun.

The other symbols used were bells, horseshoes, and stars. Of these, only the bell remains as a symbol today on modern slots. With the early slot machines, the payoffs were rather small by today's standards; a nickel for lining up two horseshoes, and the big payout, of 10 nickels, for lining up three bells.

In those days nickels as payoffs were a big inducement to play the slots. They were rather small machines, able to fit on bar tops, where they were played by the saloon's customers. They became popular immediately, for people have always loved to gamble, and in a bar atmosphere, with alcohol loosening inhibitions, it didn't take much to get the patrons gambling.

The original Liberty Bells were made of cast iron, and were manufactured by hand, one at a time. Fey was a man who liked to stay on top of things, and he ran all ends of the business, including the collection of commissions. He split the profits from the Liberty Bells with the owners of the bars, 50% to them and 50% for himself. The machines, as set by Fey, were quite lucrative and returned only 86% of the coins placed in them, giving Fey and the saloon a 14% profit.

After a while, these machines made direct cash payouts, and the Liberty Bell takes its place in history as the first three reel slot to have automatic payouts in coins. Although there had been other types of coin-operated gambling machines in use prior to Fey's invention, they were usually based on other games, such as roulette and dice, and were

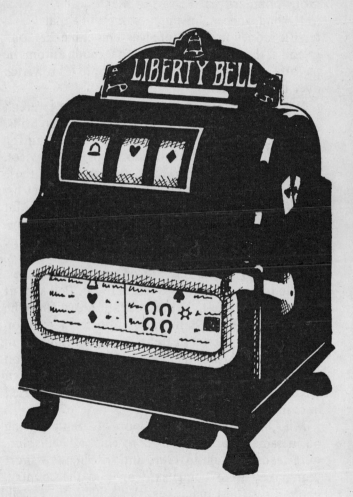

Liberty Bell Machine

rather bulky affairs. None ever achieved the enormous popularity of Fey's slot machine.

He had, indeed, invented something that was a terrific money-maker. Here was a machine that took in coins, that showed a profit, that made automatic payoffs, and didn't even need an employee to watch over its operation.

But, alas, in those days, gambling devices weren't given patents. A man named Herbert Stephen Mills, who had been in the business of manufacturing carnival games that featured coin operated devices, was intrigued by the possibilities inherent in these machines. It didn't take long for Mills to get his hands on a Liberty Bell. He then hired away Mat Larkin, who was Fey's foreman, and after much reworking and redesigning of the Fey Liberty Bell, he was in the slot machine business.

Mills didn't drive Fey out of business, however, for the original inventor of the Liberty Bell kept at his essentially one-man business all the way into the 1930s. The Liberty Bell Saloon and Restaurant on South Virginia Street in Reno, Nevada, which is run by grandsons of Charles Fey, has quite a collection of early slots. Among their collection are some of the original Liberty Bells, which are no longer used in casinos.

Mills, however, was much more of an enterprising businessman that Fey had been. The first Mills slots were ready for sale in 1906, and within a few short years, they were being sold around the country. From his earliest machines, the Mills Liberty Bell, Mills quickly moved to design and make others. The most popular of these were the High Top and Golden Falls.

The High Top and the Golden Falls were blessed with a gimmick that really made gamblers want to play them. The Mills machines took in nickels, just as the Fey Liberty Bell, but whereas the Bell nickels disappeared into the machine, never to be seen again unless there was a payout, the Mills machines were designed so that there was a window fully visible to the player, showing all the nickels already lost to the machine.

There they were, all those lovely nickels, just waiting to be paid out. It was a tremendous design feature and made the Mills machines extremely popular and successful.

In the old Liberty Bell, only one row of symbols was visible. Mills improved this feature as well. Now, a player could see three rows of symbols.

This made the game much more exciting to the players. Now, even if they lost on any particular spin, they could see how close they came to winning. If only that symbol had dropped another notch on the third row!

Mills also increased the number of symbols on each reel, to 20, giving slots the standard number that was to remain for many years. With three reels, each containing 20 symbols, the possible combinations was raised to 8,000 (20 x 20 x 20).

Another innovation credited to Mills was the use of symbols that have become standard ones for slots players in casinos all over the world. The fruit symbols, lemons, plums and cherries, and the bell and bar are ones players still see on modern machines.

Then there was another concept which still remains to this day, and that's the **jackpot,** the grand prize. It's what all slots players want to win; though today it can be in the hundreds of thousands of dollars, instead of a handful of nickels.

In the 1930s, an owner of a Mills machine was hauled into court for illegally operating a gambling device. The judge, when sentencing the man, referred to the slot machines as **one-armed bandits** and that's a term that has stuck to them to this day.

In fact, to take advantage of that term, some slots manufacturers made machines that were in the shape of gamblers, and the handle was designed as an arm, becoming a literal, instead of a figurative, *one-armed bandit.*

But neither Mills nor Fey had a monopoly on slot machines. The demand was too great and the profits too easily made for this kind of unpatentable gambling device to be kept in the hands of two men.

One of the chief competitors featured the Watling Rol-a-Top. It had an escalator window on top of the machines, showing the last eight coins inserted. It became extremely popular, not only for the players, but for the operators. The people who owned these machines liked the idea of being able to see whether recent coins inserted into the machine were slugs or the real McCoy. In the days when a nickel could buy a lunch, and men bit into half-dollars to see if they were genuine, the use of slugs was quite prevalent.

The list of manufacturers grew over the years. Names like Synder, Daval, Rock-Ola, Southern

Doll, Keeney, Evans and the Caille Brothers were common ones seen on various slot machines.

The Caille Brothers introduced a strange machine known as the Caille Gum Vendor, which was able to be placed in areas where slot machines were illegal if they paid off in coins. This machine paid off in gum instead of money, but that was a subterfuge, allowing the machine to be used without police interference. Other machines supposedly paid off in cheap candy, but when there was such a payoff, the operator of the machine exchanged coins for the candy.

Still other machines had, in addition to the usual handle, devices called **skill buttons**. These buttons were supposed to be pressed to regulate the movement of the reels, but it was all a sham and a delusion, since the pressing of the buttons had no control over the machines.

Today's machines have up to five reels and many symbols, and often are operated electronically, with all kinds of sound effects accompanying the spinning of the reels. But it's the same old "one-armed bandit" as far as casinos are concerned, because slots still provide a major source of income.

52. More About Slots

The casinos depend upon slots income for much of their profits, and continually try to upgrade their machines and the amount the gamblers will play as a basic unit. At one time, the 5¢ play, the nickel, was the standard one. This lasted all the way into the early 1970s, but even though the casino income was quite good from this 5¢ play, the executives who ran these establishments could see that they'd get five times the income if a 25¢ coin was played, and twenty times the nickel's profit if the dollar could be the standard unit of slot machine play.

To entice the bigger unit play, the casinos arranged with Bally, now the leading manufacturer of slot machines, to lease their $1 machines and make them the feature attraction in the slots area. These machines were then put into use as carousels; that is, a number of machines were arranged in an oval, with but one changeperson in the center of this oval, on an elevated perch, changing cash into dollar coins or tokens.

In order to further entice the players, the casinos lowered their profit margin on the carousels, reducing it to 5% or less. This was the first time the casinos actually stated their **edge**, or profit margin on slots they operated. If the edge was 5%, the casinos would trumpet that the $1 machines were *95% in the player's favor*. This is a bit misleading. What it really means is, that for every $100 played on the machines, the players will receive back $95. A more truthful observation would be that the machines were *5% in favor of the casino*.

But a 5% and an even lower edge, often down to 2.5%, made these machines quite attractive to slots players. As inflation moved on in the United States, the dollar wasn't worth much, and bought less and less. What was the point of winning ten nickels at an old-fashioned slot machine, when 50¢ couldn't even buy a cup of coffee in most places?

The thrill of the big jackpot, the big win at slots, was disappearing with the nickel slots. It had become a strictly penny-ante affair. The 25¢ machines had better payoffs, but not really huge jackpots. The big thrill now was reserved for the dollar slots.

To finally upgrade these machines, to get more in them, the casinos changed from a one-coin format to multiple coins. Some of the 25¢ machines required five or six coins to get all the possible payouts. On the $1 machines, at least three $1 coins had to be played to be eligible for the big jackpot.

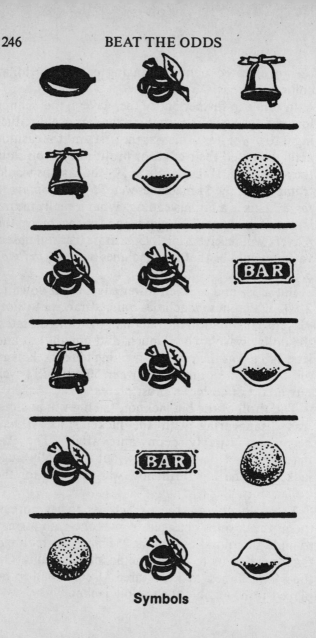

Symbols

After all these years of upgrading, the slots players now are accustomed to betting with dollars instead of nickels. There are still nickel and dime machines, to be sure, but they're taking up less and less space in the slots areas.

To run a slots area, generally all that is necessary is one employee, a changeperson, plus a slots mechanic on call. These changepersons are not only found in the casinos, but also in the drugstores, airline terminals, supermarkets and wherever else in gambling jurisdictions slots are put in. Many business owners have found that slots in their establishments are good money makers, and often spell the difference between a profitable and a losing operation. All they need is a changeperson, and in smaller establishments, where there may just be ten or fewer machines, the regular employee at the cash register could handle the change.

But the really big income on these machines is to be found in the legitimate casinos. In the more elegant ones on the Strip and in Atlantic City, the slots may provide a handsome side income, but in the smaller casinos, such as in the El Cortez or Lady Luck casinos downtown in Las Vegas, they provide the bulk of the casino's income.

And some casinos are strictly slot houses, with nothing in their establishments but slot machines. These establishments are good money makers, because the overhead, especially worker costs, are almost nil. Outside of some changepersons and a slots mechanic to take care of the machines, the casinos need no other employees.

53. Slot Machines and Slots Players

There are basically two types of slot machines. The first kind is called **straight slots**, because the payoffs are rigid and never vary. What is shown as possible payoffs on the upper part of the machine is what you get, nothing more and nothing less. These machines can be played with one coin or several coins.

Some of these machines have been upgraded to pay off on three lines, so that a minimum of three coins have to be inserted by the player to get all the possible, and usually, maximum payoffs. Others will take up to six coins, so that not only will horizontal line payoffs be possible, but diagonals will now figure in the possible payoffs.

Still other machines increase the payoffs according to how many coins are played. For example, if one coin is played, a cherry on the first reel will pay off two coins. If two coins were inserted, then four coins would be paid off. This holds true for all other payoffs on the machine. Thus, the slots player is enticed to bet six instead of one coin at a time. The more coins played, the more the player can win, but, in the long run, the casino will get bigger profits.

Then there are the **progressive** machines. These will have standard payoffs listed at the top part of the machines, but in addition to these fixed payoffs, there will be an added payoff, the big "jackpot," a progressive jackpot, increasing with every coin inserted. Depending upon the machine, the payoffs can be quite large. Obviously, there will be bigger ones at $1 machines than there will be at 25¢ or 5¢ machines.

And some of the progressive jackpots, instead of being dependent upon one machine, will have a whole cluster, bank or carousel of machines tied to a large jackpot. Anyone feeding a coin to any one of thirty machines, for example, will be increasing the progressive jackpot.

Generally, the jackpot will rise by 1¢, 5¢, or 25¢ for each coin put in. After many thousands of plays a day, the jackpot grows considerably. The jackpot on progressive machines can grow to astronomical proportions.

When a cluster of machines are involved, and these machines are fed $1 coins, the payoffs will move into the hundreds of thousands of dollars. When there's a winner, the casino executives love it, because it's great publicity for the house. The Flamingo Hilton in Las Vegas has paid out millions in these enormous jackpots. They've also taken in millions more in profits, but the players don't care about that; all they want is to be the lucky winner of that giant jackpot.

Still other machines have two progressive jackpots, each lit alternately. One may be much higher than the other, because on these machines multiple coins are encouraged, and one jackpot may be fed with more coins than the other.

When you hit one of these gigantic jackpots, a bell or other apparatus will go on, and an attendant will come over with a slot mechanic, to reset the machine. Don't, under any circumstances, play it again till you're paid off. A casino executive will verify the amount, and you'll be paid off either by check or cash.

What kind of people play the slots? Practically everyone who gambles tries their luck at them. For the most part, the serious players tend to be women, who like the thrill of gambling when they don't have to risk hundreds of dollars at a time, though with the $1 slots, that's just what they have to do sometimes.

And then there are the senior citizens, again not daring to risk too much, but hoping for the one jackpot that will ease their financial burden and put them on easy street.

There are also young people with limited cash, who want some excitement without risking too much. There are those gamblers who don't understand the table games, such as craps and blackjack, and only feel comfortable playing the slots.

In addition to these players, there are thousands

of others who have a few extra coins in their pockets and try their luck. In the Nevada gambling centers, many local residents are addicted to the slots. These "locals" do a lot of slot machine gambling in Reno, Las Vegas and other communities the length and breadth of Nevada. And they account so much for slots business that there are certain casinos that cater primarily to locals, tourists being a secondary market.

Practically everyone, sooner or later, likes to take a chance at the slots. I know a few professional poker players, proud of their skills, who never gamble at any table games. Yet, after a big win, if they have some extra money they'll cash a $20 or $50 bill and take a shot at the big progressive machines, hoping to win several thousand or much more with one pull of the handle.

Who plays slots? We all do. That's why this guide-book was written, to not only give you the flavor, the history, and the mathematics and inside story of slots, but to show you how to give it your best shot, how to win at the one-armed bandits.

54. The Mathematics of Slots

The casinos are allowed to set the slot machines to give themselves whatever percentage of profit they desire, without answering to anyone. And the best part of it, from their viewpoint, is that they don't have to tell the customers, the people actually playing the machines, just what their percentage of profit is.

And the profits are enormous. Most of the machines in the bigger casinos are tied to computers, which give the executives a readout as to profits on each machine in use. In this way, the casino executives can determine if each machine is carrying its load. If one machine is showing fewer profits, or is not profitable at all, then that machine is closed down and examined to see if it's been tampered with.

Each nickel machine gives the average Strips casino a profit of between $2,000 and $2,500 a year. If a casino has about 200 of these smaller coin machines, that's a half-million a year, clear. If most of the machines are quarter ones, then the profit is going to be approximately five times that of the nickel machines, or $10,000 to $12,500 a year. Five hundred of these quarter machines in a big Strip hotel-casino and we're talking between $5 and $7.5 million dollars a year in casino profits on slots alone.

With the slots now taking $1 coins, and with banks of them taking in the coins as fast as customers can feed the machines, and with the progressive payouts luring thousands of new customers to slots, the casinos are making a small fortune with these bigger coin slots. We've just seen what they can do with quarter machines; with the $1 ones, even with a smaller percentage of return for the casino per $100 played, the profits are substantial.

What is the usual return to the house on an average slot machine? Well, that's a hard question to answer, because the figure varies from casino to casino. All these casinos will tell you, the paying customer, is that their machines are *loose* or *"millions have been paid out over the years."* Or, *"It's 95% in your favor."*

We can grasp the 95% statement, because that means the casino is retaining 5% of all action as profits on its $1 slot machines. As to the other machines, "loose" has little real significance. What this term, loose, means to most slot players is that the machines are paying back a substantial part of the coins played. What percentage, though?

Before we go further into this situation, it would

be interesting to see just how the casino bosses set their machines and figure out their profits per machine. It's all done mathematically, and the mathematics are fairly simple and easy to follow.

The average machine uisually has three reels. And this same machine usually has twenty symbols on each reel, the cherries, watermelons, bars, etc. For our purposes, we'll examine a machine that has three reels and twenty symbols on each reel.

The first thing we want to know is how many possible combinations can be made from these three reels and twenty combinations. To do this, we multiply 20 x 20 x 20. Or 20^3. By combinations, we're referring to every possible one that can come up before they're all exhausted, such as cherry-bar-watermelon.

Multiplying this way, we come up with 8,000 possible combinations. Now we know that the handle must be pulled 8,000 times to get the full cycle of combinations played out. The casino executives know this also, and base all their profit percentages on these 8,000 spins.

They have the mechanics set the payoffs so that a certain number of coins are retained, and the number of coins divided by the 8,000 possible spins to exhaust the combinations is the profit percentage of the machine.

For example, suppose the machine, after the full cycle is finished, retains 800 coins. Then the house percentage would be 10%. If this same machine had retained 1,000 coins, then it would go up to 12.5%. If 1,200 coins were retained, it would stand at 15%, and at 20% if 1,600 coins were retained.

Now that we know this, just what is a loose machine, and, conversely, what is a *tight* machine? A loose machine would be one that retains less than 10% of the coins during any complete cycle. A tight one would hold back about 16% or more of the coins. The average Strip casino will hold back between 16% and 20% on its slots machines. These are extremely tight machines, and they're made tight because the Strip hotel-casinos cater to *high-rollers* at their table games, notably craps, blackjack and baccarat, and the slots are side profits to them.

In these casinos, the slots players are either the wives of the men playing at the table games, or tourists coming through to see the show or to look around the casinos. These are fair game for the slots in the Strip casinos. These people aren't catered to; it's the high-rollers who get all the attention and whatever they want, just so long as they're bettting big bucks.

On the other hand, the smaller casinos, those in Downtown Las Vegas and Reno, cater to the small bettor and the slot machine player. These are the customers who keep these casinos in business, and they don't want fancy frills, or opulent settings, and free champagne. They'd prefer a free pizza and beer and a good return on their slot machine action. And they're given just that by these smaller casinos.

The machines in these establishments are much looser than those in the fancy casinos. They're set to pay off a much higher return to the players, and are fixed so that they retain about 8% of the coins put in.

In other words, the house makes a good profit, but the player will get back twice as many coins as he would on the Strip.

But in the end, the casino will still retain enough to give it a handsome profit. Here, in Downtown Las Vegas, for instance, there are no heavy overhead expenses, just rows and rows of one-armed bandits, with coins seemingly falling out of every one of them in abundance. That's what the tourists who come in by bus or car from California want. That's what the "locals," the residents of Las Vegas, want.

In addition, there are other enticements. On the Strip, the casino can't be bothered with slots players, but downtown, the cocktail waitresses walk by offering free drinks and sometimes snacks; there are giveaways of money, prizes and goods. The atmosphere is made comfortable for the slots players.

While the smaller and downtown casinos will have more frequent payoffs and looser slots, they won't be involved in gigantic six- or seven-figure payouts at one time. That is left to the bigger Strip casinos. But at the downtown casinos, there will be plenty of progressive machines paying off in the thousands, but not in the hundreds of thousands. And sometimes there'll be grand prizes based on social security numbers or other gimmicks, with a compact car or RV as first prize.

We discussed the standard three-reel, twenty symbol machine in showing how the odds are figured, how the casino takes its percentage in profit. But even if you're playing a four-reel machine with twenty symbols on each reel, with 160,000 possible combinations, the house will take out the same percentage it feels comfortable with. It's as easy to set these monsters as it is to set the smaller machines.

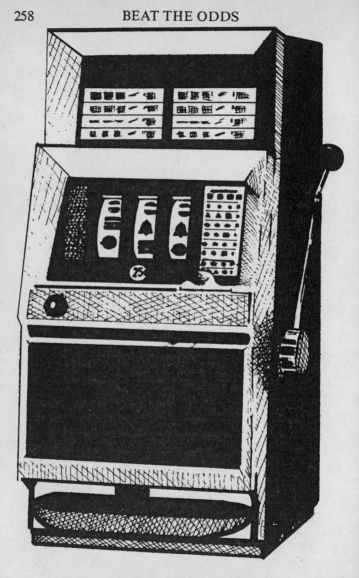

Modern Slots Machine

55. Straight, Progressive and Specialty Slots

Straight Machines

For many years, the straight slots were the only machines a gambler would play. There was a list of payoffs printed on the machine, depending upon how many of the symbols were lined up on the center row. There was also a jackpot, which never varied. If you got the three bars or whatever was necessary to line up on the center row, you won whatever the jackpot was.

But, as we've seen, the casinos were making limited profits from this idea of one coin played at a time, with one fixed payoff. It was boring as well, to pull the handle time after time, hoping for that jackpot, with no real deviations in payoffs.

The Mills machines one sees in casinos are the remnants of those times. These cast iron beauties, now aged and antiquated collector's items, still are there, especially in the smaller casinos and in Downtown Reno, where they compete against the newer slots, and still, surprisingly enough, take in their share of coins.

There are still straight slots manufactured by the leading companies that make slots, but these machines have several inducements both for the player and the house.

More than one coin can be placed in the machine for each pull. In some, as many as six are permitted. The payoffs aren't limited to the second line, but may extend to the row above and below that center. Then some machines will have diagonal as well as horizontal payoffs.

Some of these machines will pay off in proportion to the coins played; the more coins, the bigger payoff. And some will only pay off on a jackpot if the maximum number of coins permitted is played.

There'll always be action on these straight slots, but they're in the past, as newer and more enticing machines are built, with bigger payoffs and varying ways to win.

Progressive Slots

These machines have that one added feature that makes them so interesting and lucrative, and has made them the favorites of slots players the world over. In addition to the fixed payouts, these machines feature a jackpot that is progressive, that is, that keeps getting bigger the more coins are played into the machine. Thus, for each coin played a percentage of that coin is applied to the increase of the jackpot's size.

The jackpots may start at a very low figure and work their way up to a thousand dollars, or even higher, on a quarter machine. Sometimes there are two jackpots progressing along on the same machine, with each being lit alternately as the coins are put in. Some of these payoffs are quite good for a few quarter's play, if you get lucky. You can win several thousand dollars, which is a nice payday at any casino in any game.

With the $1 slots, the payoffs will run into the hundreds of thousands of dollars, and a whole bank of machines will move that jackpot along, sometimes as many as twenty or thirty machines at a time. Each coin in any of the machines will swell the jackpot's total, and any one of those machines can hit the jackpot.

These payoffs have been tremendous, and have been given enormous publicity. An unemployed actor, playing three $1 coins, hit the jackpot and collected $385,000. The dream of many people, to strike it rich with a stroke of luck, is there, embodied in these huge one-armed monsters.

These big progressive machines take a long time to get to that big jackpot, and by the time it's ripe for hitting, with a payoff of $250,000 or more, perhaps several months have passed, and millions of coins have been invested in the machines. The casino will give someone the big payout, the ultimate jackpot, but in the meantime they're getting their regular and steady profits.

A question many people ask is, "Where do all those

coins go?" Are they in the center of the machine? How many can be held there?

The next time you're in a casino, examine the slots carefully. You'll see that each rests on a table, and there's a lock in front of each table, which opens a door. What happens is this: as coins are fed into a particular machine, the innards of that machine will hold a good number of them, enough for the more modest payouts, if they should occur. But as the coins keep piling in, an automatic tripping device inside the machine releases the excess coins, and they fall through an opening into the enclosed table below the machine. Inside that table is an ordinary metal pail, which holds the coins so dropped.

Each pail is numbered to correspond to the slot machine above it, and when the pail is taken away by security guards making their rounds at collection time, a duplicate numbered pail is put in to replace the one taken out.

Then each pail's take is tallied, usually by automatic counting machines and computers, and the excess coins, removed from the pails, is what the casino counts as its profits from the slot machines.

When big payouts are to be made, usually in the thousands of dollars, a notice will be on the machine stating that for these payouts an attendant will have to be summoned. There's a bell on the machines that can be pressed to summon attendants, and a light will flash on top of the machine to show that an attendant has been called to that particular slots. After a gigantic jackpot, the machine is reset immediately at zero or wherever the jackpot started from.

Remember, there are two things you must avoid

doing when you hit a big jackpot. Mark these well in your mind.

1. If you've hit a jackpot, don't pull the handle again. Just sit there and wait for the attendant and casino executive to verify your jackpot, and to pay you off, or direct you where to be paid off. Let them pull the handle to reset the machine, but *don't touch* that handle again.

2. Some jackpots are paid off partly by coins from the machine, with the balance to be paid off by an attendant. If that's the case, don't just scoop up the coins in the well and leave. Wait for an attendant or casino executive to bring you the rest of the jackpot, which might be paid in cash or check.

These situations were most prevalent in Atlantic City when the casinos first opened. Many of the people going there were unfamiliar with casino operations and either lost their jackpots by pulling the handle again, or left their seats after collecting the coins spewed out by the machine.

The latter situation led to scams, where eagle-eyed cheats roamed the slots areas, and waited for someone to scoop up their coins and leave. Then they sat down and called for the attendant and collected the balance of the jackpot.

This led to several arrests and signs being posted to warn jackpot winners to sit tight and wait for the full payoff. And you should too. Jackpots don't come up that often, and there's no sense in not collecting what's due to you.

With the progressive slots, there won't be as many smaller payouts as on the straight machines, and there may be long periods of time between payouts.

The casino is counting on the big jackpot to entice players to these machines, players who won't mind losing their $20, $50 or $100 as long as that jackpot is viable.

Specialty Machines

Many casinos have no doors and are open day and night. This is true of several of the downtown Las Vegas and Reno houses. As a conversation piece and to draw crowds in, a few casinos have huge machines set up at these open spaces near the sidewalk.

These may be set as ordinary slots, with six or eight reels, and an exotic payoff of $10,000 or so, if one symbol lines up on all the reels. There are other, smaller payoffs available also, but the fun for the spectators is in watching the player pull a handle that may be as long as the player is, then slowly watching the symbols fall, reel by reel.

After a while, the spectators drift away, and others take their place. Some go into the casino or talk about it to the folks back home, and so, in addition to a good rake on these machines, the casinos get free advertising and walk-in customers.

These gimmick machines are seen in practically every casino in Las Vegas, though most of the plushier casinos won't put them out on the side entrance. But they're always a good conversation piece, and since casinos don't have coffee tables with the latest best sellers on them in their lobbies, these will do. And they're infinitely more profitable.

Many machines are now operated electronically, but because people get a kick out of pulling the handle, handles are supplied with the machine, though a button would do as well to get the gears in motion. Some slots can be operated by buttons instead of handles, however. But pulled or pressed, the machines are the same as to payout and house edge.

Occasionally one runs into a **double or nothing** machine, which, after a possible payout, gives the player the option of going double or nothing. And this feature goes on usually for four double or nothings.

It's a good gimmick, and allows the player to make a small killing at times. After the payoff shows on the machine, by selecting "double or nothing," the player now has a 50-50 chance on the next pull, giving the casino no advantage on this play. But to win four times in a row on the double or nothing feature is a very long-shot, and it is worthwhile to give it one chance, or possibly two, but to stop there and collect the winnings.

Not all casinos have these kinds of slots, but they're fun to play, and seem to pay off more often than ordinary machines, giving the player a constant decision, double or nothing.

These machines aren't progressive, and are of the 25¢ variety for the most part. They're not in all casinos, but can be found. Ask a security guard, or, better still, a changeperson who roams the slots area, if they're available.

56. How to Win at Slots

My mother had the best philosophy about winning at slots, but it's dull work and tends to lead to headaches and backaches. She'd go around the floor, looking into the wells of all the slots, the wells being the small metal device that holds coins falling from the machine after a win.

Occasionally she found a couple of nickels left over by a slots player. A few times she collected a bunch of quarters, and once an Ike dollar. But even my mother succumbed to the lure of the slots and with a cousin played a quarter machine, each splitting a $10 roll of quarters. After four or five spins, a $50 payoff came down, and my mother wanted to quit right then and there.

But the cousin felt that this was merely the prelude to the $1,000 jackpot that the machine was capable of, and kept putting in quarters. When the roll was exhausted, my mother insisted on splitting the $50, and took away $25, for a nice $15 profit. As I said, she wasn't much of a gambler. The cousin played his $25 out, then got another roll of $10 worth of quarters and that went also.

"I always want to quit a winner," said my mother, and that's pretty good advice for anyone to follow. The machines are set for random payoffs. What has occured before may or may not happen again, for on the average machine there are 8,000 possible combinations, and that's a lot of pulls with varying degrees of luck and bad luck, payoffs and near misses.

There's going to come a time when you're ahead on a particular machine. If you are substantially ahead, there's no more foolish feeling than giving back all the coins you've won to that same machine. Take some profits and leave. Get some coffee, take a break of some kind. Then try another machine a little later on.

Which are the best machines to play? That's a question that often is asked, and we'll try and answer it as best we can. First of all, it's not so much which machines to play, as where to play them. As we said before, there are certain casinos that cater to slots players. The machines are looser there; in addition, slots players are entitled to free soft drinks and sometimes food. And there are usually giveaways and prizes to be offered. That's where a serious slots player should head, not to a plush casino that is concerned about the high-rollers, and just uses the slots to extract as much income as they can.

But, if you're in a posh house and want to play the slots, then head for the Bally carousels where they advertise "95% or 97% in your favor." On these machines you'll be giving the house only 3% to 5% of its edge instead of the 16% they'll be raking in on the ordinary slot machines.

Sometimes these Bally slots can be played for 25¢ as well as $1. But playing them for $1 is better in the long run, than playing other slots for 25¢ where you just keep exhausting roll after roll of quarters.

In any gambling city, you'll have a choice of casinos to play in, and you can pick the ones that offer the best odds to you. If you decide to play the carousels, look at the advertising, either on the marquees or in the local papers. If one casino has a 5% edge and another only 2½% on these machines, then, all things being equal, play at the latter casino.

Then, there's another tip I can give the serious player. When you go to any carousel area, you'll notice that there's a changeperson perched on top. These changepersons are among the lowest paid employees in the casino. They rarely get tips. What you should do is ask the changeperson, when you first change your cash into dollars or quarters, which machine she recommends among those she oversees.

She'll usually suggest a particular machine, because, having nothing better to do, these employees watch to see which machines are long overdue for a jackpot. You can take her advice, which is better than going blindly to the bank of slots and picking any one at random. If you hit the big payoff, you should tip her, and thereafter, she'll always have her eye out for you and will point you to the overdue machines.

I've done that a few times with favorable results. This doesn't mean that you're going to win, but you have a shot at a machine that's long overdue, which is better than one that just paid off a big jackpot.

There is such a thing as **slot mix**, which casino

executives, but not players, are familiar with. Not only does this refer to the positioning of machines of various denominations in a slots area, but it also means setting loose and tight machines in particular orders.

Here's how this is done, and how you can take advantage of it. Most casino bosses know that people play two machines at a time; especially the serious addicts of the one-armed bandits. So, they set one machine tight and one loose. One takes and the other gives, and the casino will earn its profits. Also, loose machines are often set at aisles, generally where the crowds line up to get into the showroom. Many of these tourists are impatient with the long wait, and drift out of line to play the close slots, or can play them while standing in line.

These slots are often made loose, so that, after the tourists win some money on line, they return to that slots area to play seriously, figuring that all the machines are as loose as the one they've played at.

On straight machines, the best principle is to test a few. Don't play with money you can't afford to lose, and that will hurt you either financially or emotionally. Play for stakes you'll be comfortable with.

Try and find a machine that pays off. If you keep dropping coins into one, and it's a dud, move on. When one starts dropping coins into the well for your benefit, stick to it. If you're ahead, make sure you leave with some of your winnings intact.

While playing the progressive machines, you must realize that there'll be fewer payoffs because the casino knows you'll stick it out looking for a big jackpot. If the progressive machine has a low jackpot showing, ask a changeperson how high it gets to. There's no sense in you feeding the machine to make it payoff for someone else. Pick one that's ripe for plucking. Be patient and walk around the slots area.

You may come across two identical machines, each having progressive jackpots. On the first, the jackpot total is $354.50 and on the other $3,450.00. It's logical to go after the second machine. That one is more ripe. But, after speaking to a changeperson or someone who knows what these machines should pay off as a jackpot, if you find that they first pay off at the $5,000 mark, then move on.

Of course, a jackpot may hit at any time, but the casino wants to make a good profit and wants to delay that jackpot for as long as possible. And you want the biggest possible jackpot for your money. Even if the jackpot was completely random, it would pay to try and get $3,450 instead of $345 for your three quarters.

The same holds true for the monster payoffs. If you find that these machines don't pay off till at least $250,000 is showing on this kind of progressive jackpot, and the machine shows $186,000, no matter how enticing that figure is, go to one where the payoff is bigger. Again, you might as well get the best value for your hard-earned money. There are plenty of these colossal machines around in any legitimate gambling area. Go for the biggest, the ripest, the one that will make you most rich.

Those are the best machines to play. Avoid any in restaurants or drugstores or any business establishment. They're the tightest of all machines, and have the smallest payoffs because only a changeperson staffs them, and so she's not going to carry thousands to pay off some lucky winner.

Go to where they cater to slots players. Pick your spot. Some of these emporiums may not be to your fancy. Often a pure slot house has a lot of noise with bells going off, and lights whirling and flashing and a crowd you might not feel comfortable with. But there are others that will be more congenial. You'll get a lot of excitement and action playing the slots, why shouldn't you get the ultimate pleasure of winning as well?

Good luck.

Eight. Roulette

57. Introduction

Roulette is a game that has fascinated and intrigued millions of players over the years. It's not only a leisurely game, but an exciting game as well.

You'll be playing the same game that has attracted kings and queens, prime ministers and statesmen, millionaires and captains of industry.

Roulette has a great variety of bets available; more than in any other casino table game. Betting choices may be paid off anywhere from even-money to 35-1, and bets can be made in overlapping fashion with the same numbers covered in several ways.

Because of this factor, the game has attracted systems to beat it from the first time it was introduced. We'll show you the more popular ones and the pitfalls involved.

You'll find out about both the American and European game, including the possible wagers and payoffs involved, so that you'll be able to play this most fascinating of games intelligently.

58. American Roulette

The Dealer

In American casinos, the game is run by one dealer. This is in contrast to the European version of roulette in which several **croupiers** (the French term for dealer) are used, for the European game is played with a double layout, and more employees are needed to staff the table.

But in American casinos, one dealer will suffice to run the game. Sometimes, if the game is particularly busy, the dealer may have an assistant, whose sole function will be to collect losing chips and stack them up. But this is the exception, rather than the rule.

The dealer has several duties. He or she will first change the player's cash into roulette chips. Each player will receive roulette chips of a different color from the other players' chips. These roulette chips have no intrinsic value away from the roulette table and are specially marked. The different colors make for a smoother game, since there will usually be a multitude of bets on the layout, and the only way the dealer will know how to make proper payoffs will be through the color of the chips.

In addition to changing cash for chips, the dealer runs the game. He keeps the wheel in spin, and spins a small white ball counter to the wheel's motion, rolling this ball and letting it spin away till it falls into a slot on the wheel. This slot determines the winning number and other payoffs.

After a winning number is determined, the dealer collects all the losing chips first, and then pays off the winning bets. After this is done, the players make bets prior to the next spin of the ball, and the whole procedure begins again.

There is usually a pitboss in the vicinity of the roulette wheel. He or she may supervise the play at the roulette table and will be called upon in case there is a dispute between the players and the dealer or if the players themselves disagree. But this rarely happens when all the players use different colored roulette chips.

Roulette Chips

As we mentioned, the chips are in different colors and are marked differently than other casino chips. A player can't wager them at any other game in the casino. Not only that, but players are forbidden from taking these chips away from the roulette table. When they've finished playing, they must turn in all their chips to the dealer, who will pay off the player by exchanging these for casino chips, which can then be brought to the cashier's cage and exchanged for cash.

There is usually a standard value placed on the roulette chips. In the old days, before inflation, 10¢ or 25¢ chips were the standard. Today, it's hard to find a standard chip value less than $1. If a player gives the dealer a $20 bill he or she will receive 20 chips, each having a standard value of $1. However, the player is not stuck with this value.

Suppose that a player came with a $100 bill and wanted each chip to be valued at $5. This will be done, and the dealer, to make certain that there is no mistake, will place that colored chip on the outside rim of the wheel with a $5 marker on it, or a button to show that a stack of 20 chips is worth $100.

Where no chips are on the rim, everyone is playing with the standard value chips. These chips will come in enough colors, usually eight or ten different ones, to accommodate that many players. There will also be enough chairs at the roulette table for this many players.

Players may change the valuation of their chips. If a player won a lot of money, rather than betting handfuls of $1 chips, he may change the valuation to $5 for his colored chips, by turning them in, and getting them re-valued, or getting different colored chips. He or she may not want to bet standard casino chips of that same valuation, since there may be a problem if another player is also betting casino chips, and there may be a dispute as to who is entitled to a payoff. The same holds true for cash bets, which we don't recommend using.

For bigger bets, casino chips of the regular kind can be used. This is for $5, $25 and $100 bets. However, the vast majority of bets will be made by using the roulette chips.

When payoffs are made, the dealer **cuts** the chips, that is, he breaks into the stacks of chips at his disposal. If the payoff is 17 chips, for example, he'll cut a 20 stack by taking away three chips from that stack and moving them by hand to the winner.

This is in contrast to the European game where a **rake** is used to collect and pay off chips. In both games, after the number has come up, some kind of marker is placed on the layout to indicate the winning number before the losing chips are collected and winning bets are paid off.

The American Wheel

The game of roulette depends on the spin of the wheel, an ornate device that is approximately three feet in diameter and contains slots numbered from 1 to 36, plus a 0 and 00.

The bowl of the wheel, which takes up most of the space on a roulette wheel contains numbered pockets. Above this are eight metal buffers, some horizontal and some vertical, which are there to slow down the ball as it spins counter to the wheel's motion, so that it will fall into a pocket in the most random manner possible.

When it falls into a pocket, that pocket corresponds to a particular number, and that number determines which bets win and which lose for that spin of the wheel.

Each pocket is separated from its neighbors by metal dividers, which are known as separators. As the ball slows down, it may fall into a pocket only to bounce up and into another pocket, but eventually its inertia will cause it to remain in one pocket. That pocket contains a number, and that's the winning number for that spin.

There are 36 numbers in all, half in black and half in red, plus two extra numbers, the 0 and 00, which are in green. The numbers aren't in consecutive order on the wheel, but are placed randomly, with red and black numbers alternating, except when broken up by the 0 and 00.

With thirty six numbers on the wheel, half will be odd and half even, half will be black and half red, and half will be in the lower tier (1-18) and half in the higher tier (19-36). All of these are possible bets; odd-even, red-black, and high-low, and as we shall see, are paid off at even-money.

If there were only 36 numbers, then the house would have no advantage over the player, and it would be merely a game of chance without either side, the bettor or casino, having an edge. However, the addition of the 0 and 00 gives the house a definite advantage of 5.26%. These could be called *house numbers,* because they are winning numbers for the house when the player bets on any of the even-money propositions just mentioned, as well as on other numbers and betting propositions.

A gambler could bet on the 0 and 00 as a number,

The American Wheel

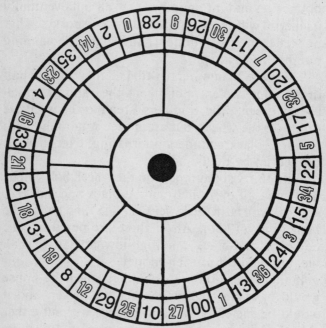

as well as any other numbers, but then it means that there are 38 possible numbers to bet on, with the payoff at 35-1 on a single number, still giving the casino a 5.26% advantage.

Since the house has a built-in advantage, it wants the game played as honestly as possible, and therefore the roulette wheels are built as friction-free as possible, so that there is no **bias** or deviation from a random situation prevailing. The wheels are inspected frequently and checked out for any worn parts, such as pockets or dividers, for these may create such a bias.

Some players go from wheel to wheel, clocking them and checking out the pattern of numbers that come up, hoping for such a bias, but it is rarely found. If more numbers come up in any sequence out of the ordinary, it is more probably coincidence, for when there's a random sampling, numbers can repeat and come up in strange sequences, and the spins can still be the result of chance.

The Roulette Layout

Now we come to the partner of the wheel at the roulette table, the layout. The layout contains all the possible betting situations that a player can have while playing roulette. The following is a typical roulette layout.

The layouts are usually in green. The numbers from 1 through 36 are divided into three columns,

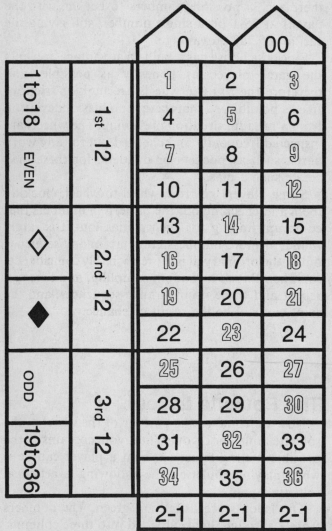

The Layout

and are in numerical order. Each one is either red or black, corresponding to the colors on the wheel. 0 and 00 are at the head of the columns of numbers, and may be bet upon separately or together.

On the outside are the **even-money** bets, 1-18, Even, red, black, odd and 19-36. Between them and the columns are the **dozens bets**, 1-12, 13-24 and 25-36, placed so that they correspond with the numbers in the columns. On the layout these dozens bets are marked 1st 12, 2nd 12 and 3rd 12.

Finally we have the **columns bets**, which are at the far end of the columns, opposite the 0 and 00 areas. They each show 2-1, and are paid off at that price. Each of these column areas covers all the numbers running down the column.

This is the standard layout to be found in American casinos, and as we have said, it will accommodate all the possible bets that can be made at the game of roulette.

59. Inside Bets

The bets we'll be discussing in this section could be called **inside** bets, since they take place within the 1-36 numbers plus the 0 and 00. With the exception of one bet, the Five-Number bet, which gives the house a 7.89% advantage, all the following wagers in American roulette give the house an edge of 5.26%

Inside Bets

3	6	9	12	15	18	21	24	27	30	33	36
2	5	8	11	14	17	20	23	26	29	32	35
1	4	7	10	13	16	19	22	25	28	31	34

Let's begin with a favorite of roulette players the world over.

Straight-Up Bets

Single Number Bet — Pays 35-1.

When a chip is placed on a single number, as shown on the layout with a chip placed in number 3, this is known as a straight-up wager, and if the number comes up, the payoff is 35-1. If any other number comes up, including 0 and 00, the bet is lost.

Straight-Up Bets

A single number bet can be made on any number on the layout, including numbers 1-36, plus 0 and 00. No matter what number he places the chip on, the payoff will be the same, at 35-1.

A player is not limited to one straight-up bet. He may make as many as he desires, and place as many chips on a single number (up to the house limit) as he or she desires. For example, a player can put five chips on number 0, two on number 4, and one each on numbers 12, 15, 23 and 34. It is up to the inclinations of the player. No one will object, and since your chips will have a special roulette color, they'll easily be identified as yours, and you'll be paid off.

To bet correctly, place your chip in the center of the numbered box, being careful not to touch any of the surrounding lines. If you touch the lines, you might have another kind of bet.

If another bettor likes your number and has

placed a chip in that box, that doesn't foreclose you from making the same bet. Simply place your chip on the bettor's chip. Or you may place several chips on the bettor's chip. This is perfectly valid. The house edge on this bet is 5.26%.

Split Bets

Two-Number Bet — Pays 17-1.

In order to make a split bet, you should place your chip on the line between two contiguous or adjacent numbers. On the layout, we see the chip placed between numbers 6 and 9 as a split bet, covering both numbers. Also, the chip between 5 and 6 is a split bet.

Split Bets

If either number comes up on a split bet, the player wins at 17-1. Split bets give the player double the chance to win, at half the payoff. Any two numbers may be split, as long as there is a line separating them. In addition, 0 and 00 may be bet as a split number, either by putting a chip between these numbers, or putting one on the line between the second and third dozens, when a player can't reach the 0 and 00 box.

Trio Bets

Three Number Bet   Pays 11-1.

A trio bet can be made by placing a chip on the line separating the dozens betting area from the columns of numbers. Thus, the chip on the number 13 line on the layout will cover the numbers 13, 14 and 15.

Trio Bets

When making a trio bet, the player will have three consecutive numbers covered, and will be paid 11-1 if any of those numbers come up on the wheel.

As you can see by the layout, the numbers that can be covered with a trio bet include 1, 2 and 3; 10, 11 and 12; 25, 26 and 27, to show but three other examples.

The house advantage on this bet is still 5.26%.

Corner Bets

Four-Number Bet   Pays 8-1.

This bet is made when a chip is placed at the point where all four numbers converge, right in that corner, as the chip placed between numbers 23, 24, 26 and 27 shows. Now, if any of those numbers come up on the next spin of the wheel, the payoff will be 8-1. This is a pretty versatile wager and can be used to cover various groups of four numbers, such as 2, 3, 5 and 6; 7, 8, 10 and 11; 22, 23, 25 and 26; 32, 33, 35, and 36, as examples.

Corner Bets

The corner bet gives the house the usual 5.26% advantage.

Five-Number Bet

Five-Numbers Bet   Pays 6-1.

This wager can only be made one way, and it covers the numbers 0, 00, 1, 2 and 3. It is made by placing the chip at the convergence of the line separating the 0 and 00, with the line separating these numbers from the 1, 2, and 3. However, after noting where the chip goes, forget about this bet, for one very good reason. It gives the house an advantage of 7.89%, and is the **worst bet** on the entire roulette layout.

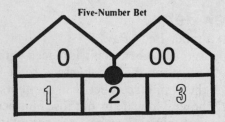

Five-Number Bet

Since the French wheel, which contains only O, doesn't have the 00, this bet can't be made on that wheel. So, remember our advice, and never make a five-number bet on the American wheel.

Six-Number Bet

Six-Numbers   Pays 5-1.

As we can see from the layout diagram, the chip for this wager should be placed on the outside line separating the dozens bets from the inside numbers, at a point where this line crosses a line perpendicular to it, separating the six numbers we want to bet on.

Six-Number Bet

In the diagram, this chip is placed so that the numbers 28, 29, 30, 31, 32 and 33 are covered. Thus one chip covers all six numbers, and if any of the numbers hit, then the bet will be paid off at 5-1.

There are eleven possible ways to make this six-number bet running up and down the side of the layout. Since it covers so many numbers at one time, with a good 5-1 payoff, it's a popular bet.

The house edge on this wager is 5.26%.

A final note on these wagers: No matter how they're made and for how many chips, if the five-number wager is avoided, then the house edge will never be more nor less than 5.26%.

With all of these wagers, the player may make several bets of the same kind, covering several numbers, and combinations of bets, covering as many numbers as he or she wishes, with as many chips as he or she desires to bet, provided that it is within the house limit on wagers.

60. Outside Bets

The bets we'll now cover take place outside the 1-36 and 0, 00 numbered area, and are therefore considered **outside wagers.**

There are three types of bets here. First there are the even-money wagers, then the dozens bets and finally the column bets. We'll discuss each in turn.

Outside Bets

1st 12		2nd 12		3rd 12	
1to18	EVEN	◇	◆	ODD	19to36

The Even-Money Bets

There are three possible types of bets that can be made at even-money; high-low, odd-even or red-black. Of course, a player can make wagers on each of these choices, betting, for example, odd, red and high.

Even-Money Bets

1 to 18	EVEN	◇	◆	ODD	19 to 36

When betting on even-money choices, the house wins automatically if the ball lands in the 0 or 00. There's one exception to this, and this takes place in Atlantic City, or wherever else there's a **surrender** rule.

Let's discuss this now. If the number coming up is 0 or 00, where surrender is allowed, the casino will allow you to remove **one-half of your bet**. In other words, you're surrendering half your bet.

In the European casinos they go one step further. In those casinos, there is the **en prison** rule. You can either surrender half your bet, or allow your bet to be **imprisoned for one more spin.** If your choice then comes up, your bet stays intact. You won't win but at least you have your bet back. In Atlantic City you just get surrender, however.

In the Nevada casinos, neither rule is in force. So, if you bet on any even-money choice and the 0 or 00 comes up, you're out of luck. You lose your chip or chips outright.

High-Low Bets

The first of the even-money bets we'll discuss is high-low. You can bet high (19-36) or low (1-18). If you bet high and any number from 19 to 36 comes up, you win your bet at even-money, or 1-1. If you bet low and any number from 1-18 comes up, you win that bet, also at even-money.

High-Low Bet

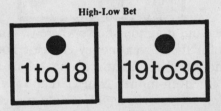

Odd-Even

If you bet odd, then if any odd number comes up on the next spin of the wheel, you win your wager at even-money, or 1-1. If you bet even, then if any even number comes up, you bet is paid off at even-money. Remember, however, that the numbers 0 and 00 are losers for this kind of bet, as they are for all even-money bets.

Odd-Even Bet

Red-Black

There are 18 red numbers and 18 black numbers, so the chances of a red or black number coming up

on the next spin of the wheel are equal. If you bet on
red, then you will be paid off at even-money, or 1-1 if
a red number comes up. If you bet black, then you
win if a black number comes up at even-money.

Red-Black Bet

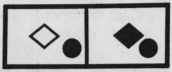

The layout diagram shows where you make your
wagers for these even-money choices. You can bet
any amount up to the house limit, which is usually
higher for even-money choices than for the inside
numbers, because the payoff is only at even-money.

These even-money choices are the heart of many
roulette systems, and we'll cover a few in the later
sections of this book, showing how they work, as
well as their pitfalls.

Dozens Bets

These bets are paid off at 2-1, and there are three
ways to bet them. You can bet on the first dozen, the
second dozen or the third dozen. The first dozen
covers numbers from 1-12 and is often called on
layouts, the **1st 12**. The numbers from 13-24 is the
second dozen and is known as the **2nd 12**. Finally
the third dozen, from 25-36 is known as the **3rd 12**.
For each of those bets, you are covering 12 numbers.
Some players bet on two dozens at one time, giving
themselves 24 numbers. But on these bets, as on the
even-number wagers and the columns wagers, the
house edge is always 5.26%.

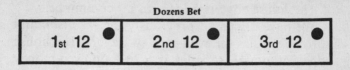

Dozens Bet

1st 12 ●	2nd 12 ●	3rd 12 ●

When a 0 or 00 comes up, you have an automatic loser. These numbers aren't included in the dozens bets, and there is no surrender or *en prison* rule covering them in any casino.

The layout diagram shows just how to make these wagers, and where to place the chip or chips you bet. The house limit on these bets is higher than those on the inside numbers.

Columns Bet

These bets are made at the head of each column directly opposite on the layout from 0 and 00. A bet on a particular column covers 12 numbers, some red and some black.

Columns Bet

3	6	9	12	15	18	21	24	27	30	33	36	2-1 ●
2	5	8	11	14	17	20	23	26	29	32	35	2-1 ●
1	4	7	10	13	16	19	22	25	28	31	34	2-1 ●

The payoff is at 2-1 for each column bet, but the 0 and 00 aren't included in any column. If they come up, the column bet is lost, for there is no surrender or *en prison* rule on column wagers.

The house edge is 5.26% on all column bets.

We have discussed previously the *en prison* and surrender rules on even-money wagers. The house edge without these rules is 5.26% on even-money and on the dozens and columns bets. With the *en prison* and surrender rules, the house advantage drops to 2.70% **only on the even-money wagers.**

Chart 1
Recapitulation of Bets and Payoffs

Single Number	35-1
Two Numbers	17-1
Three Numbers	11-1
Four Numbers	8-1
Five Numbers	6-1
Six Numbers	5-1
Column	2-1
Dozen	2-1
Odd-Even *	1-1
Red-Black *	1-1
High-Low *	1-1

All of the above bets give the house an advantage of 5.26%, except for the five-numbers bet, which gives the casino an advantage of 7.89%.

* When the surrender feature is allowed, the house advantage on these bets drops to 2.70%.

61. European Roulette

The European game and the American game are nearly the same. The main difference, besides the use of French terms, is in the use of but a single zero in the European game, while the American wheel has a zero and a double zero. There is also the **en prison** rule used in the European game. Both the **en prison** rule and the single zero are beneficial to the players, and bring the casino advantage down to 1.35%.

The following is a French wheel:

The French Wheel

This wheel has spaces for 37 numbers, the numerals 1-36 and the 0. Red and black numbers alternate, but the placement of numbers is different than the American wheel.

Like the American wheel, there is a groove near the rim of the wheel where the croupier places the ball, spinning it counter to the action of the wheel, to give it the most random kind of spin. Then it hits metal buffers as it loses velocity, and finally falls into one of the pockets, which is separated from the other pockets by metal sides.

The Layout

The following is a French layout used in the European and English casinos.

It differs from the American layout in that the even money choices are on opposite sides, and the dozens bets can be made on two different sides. The wheel is to the top of the box showing the 0.

The European Layout

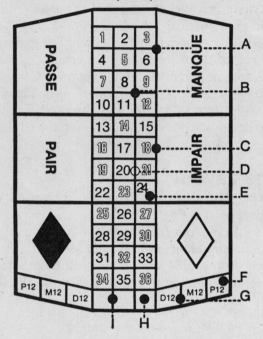

The European Layout

A. Transversale	6	numbers.
B. Carre	4	numbers.
C. Transversale	3	numbers.
D. Cheval	2	numbers.
E. Number, *en plein*	1	number.
F. Dozen	12	numbers.
G. Two dozens	24	numbers.
H. Column	12	numbers.
I. Two columns	24	numbers.

Let's compare the European and American bets, showing the different nomenclature.

Chart 2 European and American Nomenclature		
American Bet	**French Term**	**Odds**
Straight-Up (One Number)	En plein	35-1
Split (Two Numbers)	A cheval	17-1
Trio (Three Numbers)	Transversale	11-1
Corner (Four Numbers)	Carre	8-1
Six Numbers	Sixain	5-1
* Red-Black	Rouge-Noir	1-1
* High-Low	Passe-Manque	1-1
* Odd-Even	Impair-Pair	1-1
Column	Colonne	2-1
Dozen	Douzaine	2-1

* The *en prison* rule is in effect for these betting choices only.

When making the dozen bets, you should realize that the first dozen (1-12) is marked as **P12** on the layout, standing for **Premiere**. The second dozen (13-24) is called **M12** for **Moyenne** meaning middle. The third dozen is **D12** for **Derniere**, or last.

The *en prison* rule can be summarized as follows: When a 0 comes up on the wheel, the player's bet isn't lost. He or she has two choices. First, he or she can surrender half the wager made, which is known as **partage**, and take off the other half of the bet. Or the bet can be imprisoned for another spin and if it wins, then the bet is whole, but nothing else is won. To differentiate this wager from the ordinary wager, the chip or chips are placed on the line that borders the betting area.

Since the house advantage with the *en prison* rule is 1.35%, the most advantageous bets for the players would be on the even-money choices when playing in a European casino.

There are many special bets available at European casinos, mostly involving what the French call **voisins**, or neighbors. These can be the *voisins* of any particular number on the wheel, which includes the number and two numbers on either side, making it a five-chip bet.

There is the **voisins du zero**, which is a nine-chip bet, with eight chips bet on splits and one chip on the trio, 0-2-3.

There are other wagers that are special to the European wheel, such as **finals, les tiers** and **les orphelins**, which are rather complicated. We would advise the player to concentrate instead on the even-money choices and the simpler bets, such as corner bets or splits.

62. Strategies and Systems at Roulette

Because of the high house edge at the American wheel without the surrender rule (5.26%) this is not a game that you might want to play for very serious money. The house advantage is very strong and quite difficult to overcome in the long run.

Therefore, limit your losses, and if you find yourself winning, try to make a good score and then quit winners. That kind of philosophy can't be beat when gambling.

Getting Your Roulette Chips

When you come to the table, you should first inquire of the dealer just what the minimum bets are at the table. If they're too high for your pocketbook, then don't play at that table. **Don't gamble with money you can't afford to lose, either financially or emotionally.**

Different casinos have different minimum bet limits. And they have different standard valuations for their chips. Some casinos will have a 25¢ value as a standard value. This means that a stack of 20 chips will cost you $5. This is the way to figure out the basic valuations; find out what a stack of chips will cost you.

Some casinos will have 50¢, $1 or even higher valuations placed on their chips. At 50¢ a chip, a stack will cost you $10. $1 chips will set you back $20 for a stack of 20 chips.

If you feel comfortable with the amount of money you're going to risk, then the next question you want to ask the dealer is this: What is the minimum bet allowed for the inside as well as the outside numbers. The inside numbers are all those numbers, from 1-36 plus the 0 and 00, that can be bet as one, two, three, four or six number bets. The outside bets are those that pay off at even-money, plus the dozen and column wagers.

Even though the chips cost 25¢ each, the casino might require a minimum outside bet of $1, and an inside minimum bet of 25¢ on any choice but with at least four chips in play at one time. In other words, you can't just place down one chip on an inside betting proposition. You'll have to put down at least four on one or several betting choices and that means risking a dollar.

This is fairly standard in casinos. So make certain that your bankroll can handle it. If you're at a table with a $1 valuation for the chips, and you must bet four (and sometimes five) chips at one time on the inside propositions, then with a few losses you're going to be out of your original stake.

What Bets to Make

If you're playing at a standard American table, with the 0 and 00 and no surrender, then all your bets will give the house the same advantage of 5.26%. That is, except for the five-number wager (0, 00, 1, 2 and 3) which we don't advise making.

The higher the odds, the less likely you'll win. The lower the odds, the more often you'll have wins. Thus, if you bet only on single numbers as straight-up bets, you'll get 35-1 for a win, but the odds are 37-1 against this happening.

On the other hand, if you bet on the even-money choices, the odds against winning on these are only 20-18 against. You have 18 numbers working for you, but 20 against you, including the 0 and 00. Obviously you will theoretically win 18 out of 38 times, much better than 1 out of 37 times when betting a straight-up number.

However, the payoff is much less, only even-money. Therefore, you must use your discretion when making bets. Are you the type that wants to take a shot at a big payoff, or do you want to conserve your betting capital and hope to get a little ahead? It's your choice; the odds are the same as far as house percentage goes.

There are ways to compromise. You can make six-number bets and cover a large variety of numbers and still get a good payoff. You can bet a key number, and bet it straight-up, surrounding it with corner and trio bets. All kinds of possibilities are available at the roulette table. Again, the choice is yours.

When playing at a table that allows surrender, then by all means concentrate on the even-money betting propositions. They cut the house edge in half, and why not take advantage of this? The same holds true when betting in a European game. Bet on the even-money choices. You get a second chance at winning back your bet when a 0 shows. And the house edge on this bet is down to 1.35%.

Betting Systems

The most well-known, and the most treacherous systems to play are the Martingale and the Grand Martingale. The Martingale is often played by novices who feel that sooner or later their choice is going to come up, and to rationalize their bets, they call upon the *law of averages*.

Here's how the Martingale system works. It's really nothing more than a doubling up system. After a loss, you double your bet till you win. For example, let's suppose you bet $1. You lose. Then you bet $2. You lose. You bet $4. You lose. You bet $8 and win.

Having won, you start all over again with a $1 wager. How much can you win with this system? Well, when you finish a sequence of doubling up with a win, you are ahead $1 only. Here's why.

Bet	Loss
$1	$1
$2	$3
$4	$7

At this point, you're behind $7. Then you bet $8 and win, and so you're ahead $1. Even if the bets escalate to $16, $32, $64 $128 and $256, when you finally win, you win $1. Imagine betting $256 to win $1! But that's what this system is all about.

The Grand Martingale is even tougher. After each loss you add a unit to the bet, so that you win more than $1 when you finally win. But the loss sequence is $1, $3, $7, $15 and so forth, and this can lead to astronomical losses in a very short time. Avoid this system as well.

The systems players who are die-hards think that the doubling up method will win because of the law of averages. So, after they've lost five bets on red, they feel red is overdue because of the *law of averages*.

What they don't know is that there is no law of averages. There is the law of large numbers, which roughly states that the more events played the closer to the theoretical norm will be the result.

Thus, at the time the systems player is hoping for red to come up, he doesn't know that after a million spins of the wheel (excluding the 0 and 00) red has come up 521,202 and black has come up 478,798 and black still has a long way to go to catch up. It may never catch up, but will come closer to the 50% norm as time goes by, and there are several more million spins of the wheel.

If you want to play a betting system, play a very conservative one. For example, you might bet $1 and if it loses, bet $2. If that loses, you just want to get even, so you bet $3. If that loses, you've lost $6 and stop, and start again with a $1 bet, hoping to win enough times during the first two spins to make up for the loss. Of course, you're not going to get rich that way. But you won't be losing your bankroll with one bad run of luck.

Since roulette is a leisurely game where you can sit down comfortably and make bets between spins of the wheel without much pressure, we'd sugggest that you buy two stacks of chips and have fun playing, hoping by luck to make some money.

Therefore, our best advice would be to play some favorite numbers, make some corner bets and perhaps a few even-number wagers. Enjoy yourself. With some luck, you could win big.

63. Money Management

This is always important in gambling. It means managing your gambling stake so that it not only can last a long time, but will give you the chance of winning. For purposes of playing roulette, we'd suggest getting two stacks of chips only if you can afford to take this risk. Play with the standard valuations. Now you have 40 chips to bet. To make them last, you might pick a few favorite numbers and cover them with corner or six-number bets, to give yourself a good chance of picking up a winning number. At the same time, place a chip on two favorite numbers. If they hit, you're getting 35-1.

Try and double your stake. If you do that, you're doing well at roulette. You've made a nice win, and it's time to leave the table. If your luck turns the other way and you lose, then don't reach into your pocket for more cash. Set your loss limits when you sit down at the table. Two stacks and that's all you'll lose.

In this way, you'll have a shot at winning some money, have some fun gambling, and it won't cost you that much if you lose.

Good luck!

64. Glossary

American Wheel—The roulette wheel containing a 0 and 00.

Ball—The white ball used in roulette, which is made of plastic, spun against the wheel's rotation to give a random spin.

Column Bet—A bet on one of the three columns on the roulette layout, each of which contains 12 numbers, and is paid off at 2-1.

Combination Bet—A wager such as a corner bet, covering several numbers on the inside with the use of one chip.

Corner Bet—An inside bet using one chip to cover four numbers at one time. Also known as a **Four-Numbers Bet**.

Croupier—The French term for the employee who runs the roulette game.

Double Zero—See **Zero**.

Dozen Bet—A wager on either the first, second, or third dozen numbers on the layout.

En Prison Rule—When a 0 or 00 comes up, the player has the option of giving up half his bet or imprisoning the bet for one more spin. If the player's choice comes up then, the bet is not lost.

Even-Money Choices—Bets paid off at even-money, which include **High-Low, Odd-Even,** and **Red-Black.**

Five-Number Bet—A wager covering the 0, 00, 1, 2 and 3 which pays off at 6-1 and gives the house an advantage of 7.89%.

French Wheel—The standard wheel used in Europe containing but a single zero.

High-Low Bet—An even-money bet that the next spin will come up either high (19-36) or low (1-18), depending on whether the bettor has wagered on high or low.

Inside Bet—A wager on any of the numbers, or combinations of the numbers, including 0 and 00.

Layout—The printed surface showing all the wagers that can be made in roulette, on which players place their bets.

Martingale System—A doubling up system after each loss.

Odd-Even Bet—An even-money wager that the next spin will come up the way the player bet it, either an odd or even number.

Outside Bet—A wager on either the dozens, columns or even-money choices.

Red-Black Bet—A wager paid off at even-money on either the red or black numbers.

Six-Numbers Bet—A bet covering six inside numbers with one chip.

Split Bet—A bet covering two numbers with one chip, paying off at 17-1.

Straight-Up Bet—A wager on one particular number on the layout, which pays off at 35-1.

Trio Bet—An inside bet covering three numbers at one time with one chip.

Voisons—The French term for neighbors, referring to neighboring numbers on the French wheel.

Zero, Double Zero—Numbers on the wheel in addition to the regular 1-36 numerals, which allow the casino to have an edge over the players.

Nine.
One Final Word

Well, there you have it, a world of information presented to you on how to win at gambling. We gamble not only to enjoy ourselves, but to win as well, and if our advice is followed, we'll be doing more of both every time we place our bets. After all, winning is more fun.

However, you must remember to gamble intelligently, and never to risk money if the losing of such money hurts you financially or emotionally. We're gambling to be winners, and we mean that in more ways than one. This book is not written to encourage gambling, but rather to make you as informed as possible and give you every chance to make the best bets possible and be a winner.

No matter what game you intend to play, one or all, we hope that our book has helped you become a better player, and that now, armed with powerful information, you will be a winner at gambling.

Let's beat the odds!

313

Baccarat Master Card Counter
NEW WINNING STRATEGY!

For the **first time,** Gambling Research Institute releases the **latest winning techniques** at baccarat. This **exciting** strategy, played by big money players in Monte Carlo and other exclusive locations, is based on principles that have made insiders and pros **hundreds of thousands of dollars** counting cards at blackjack - card counting!

NEW WINNING APPROACH

This brand **new** strategy now applies card counting to baccarat to give you a **new winning approach,** and is designed so that any player, with just a little effort, can successfully take on the casinos at their own game - and win!

SIMPLE TO USE, EASY TO MASTER

You learn how to count cards for baccarat without the mental effort needed for blackjack! No need to memorize numbers - keep the count on the scorepad. Easy-to-use, play the strategy while enjoying the game!

LEARN WHEN TO BET BANKER, WHEN TO BET PLAYER

No longer will you make bets on hunches and guesses - use the GRI Baccarat Master Card Counter to determine when to bet Player and when to bet Banker. You learn the basic counts (running and true), deck favorability, when to increase bets and much more in this **winning strategy.**

LEARN TO WIN IN JUST ONE SITTING

That's right! After **just one sitting** you'll be able to successfully learn this powerhouse strategy and use it to your advantage at the baccarat table. Be the best baccarat player at the table - the one playing the odds to **win!** Baccarat can be beaten. The Master Card Counter shows you how!

FREE BONUS!

Order now to receive **absolutely free,** The Basics of Winning Baccarat. One quick reading with this great primer shows you how to play and win.

To order, send $50 by bank check or money order to:

Cardoza Publishing.P.O. Box 1500, Cooper Station, New York, NY 10276

PROFESSIONAL VIDEO POKER STRATEGY
Win at Video Poker - With the Odds!

At last, for the first time, and for serious players only, the GRI Professional Video Poker strategy is released so you too can play to win! You read it right - this strategy gives you the mathematical advantage over the casino and what's more, it's easy to learn!

PROFESSIONAL STRATEGY SHOWS YOU HOW TO WIN WITH THE ODDS
This powerhouse strategy, played for big profits by an exclusive circle of professionals, people who make their living at the machines, is now made available to you! You too can win - with the odds - and this winning strategy shows you how!

HOW TO PLAY FOR A PROFIT
You'll learn the key factors to play on a pro level: which machines will turn you a profit, break-even and win rates, hands per hour and average win per hour charts, time value, team play and more! You'll also learn big play strategy, alternate jackpot play, high and low jackpot play and key strategies to follow.

WINNING STRATEGIES FOR ALL MACHINES
This comprehensive, advanced pro package not only shows you how to win money at the 8-5 progressives, but also, the winning strategies for 10s or better, deuces wild, joker's wild, flat-top, progressive and special options features.

BE A WINNER IN JUST ONE DAY
In just one day, after learning our strategy, you will have the skills to consistently win money at video poker - with the odds. The strategies are easy to use under practical casino conditions.

BONUS - PROFESSIONAL PROFIT EXPECTANCY FORMULA ($15 VALUE)
For serious players, we're including this bonus essay which discusses the profit expectancy principles of video poker and how to relate them to real dollars and cents in your game.

To order, send $50 by check or money order to Cardoza Publishing

316

THE CARDOZA CRAPS MASTER
Three Big Strategies!
Exclusive Offer! - Not Available Anywhere Else

Here It is! **At last**, the **secrets** of the **Grande-Gold Power Sweep, Molliere's Monte Carlo Turnaround** and the **Montarde-D'Girard Double Reverse** - three big strategies - are made available and presented for the **first time anywhere!** These powerful strategies are designed for the serious craps player, one wishing to bring the best odds and strategies to hot tables, cold tables and choppy tables.

1. The Grande-Gold Power Sweep (Hot Table Strategy)

This **dynamic strategy** takes maximum advantage of hot tables and shows the player methods of amassing small **fortunes quickly** when numbers are being thrown fast and furious. The Grande-Gold stresses aggressive betting on wagers the house has no edge on! This previously unreleased strategy will make you a powerhouse at a hot table.

2. Molliere's Monte Carlo Turnaround (Cold Table Strategy)

For the player who likes betting against the dice, **Molliere's Monte Carlo** Turnaround shows how to turn a cold table into hot cash. Favored by an exclusive circle of professionals who will play nothing else, the uniqueness of this strongman strategy is that the vast majority of bets **give absolutely nothing away to the casino!**

3. The Montarde-D'Girard Double Reverse (Choppy Table Strategy)

This **new** strategy is the **latest** and **most exciting development** in recent years. **Learn how** to play the optimum strategies against the tables when the dice run hot and cold (a choppy table) with no apparent reason. **The Montarde-d'Girard Double Reverse** shows you how you can **generate big profits** while less knowledgeable players are ground out by choppy dice. And, of course, the majority of our bets give nothing away to the casino!

BONUS!!! - Order now, and receive **The Craps Master-Professional Money Management Formula** ($15 value) **absolutely free!** Necessary for serious players and **used by the pros**, it features the unique **stop-loss ladder**

To order send ~~$75~~ $50 by check or money order to: <u>Cardoza Publishing,</u>

318